THE MAN IN THE MANSE

THE MAN IN THE MANSE

RONALD S. BLAKEY

The Handsel Press Limited
1978

Published by
The Handsel Press Ltd.
33 Montgomery Street, Edinburgh

ISBN 0 905312 05 8

First published 1978

Printed in Great Britain by
R. & R. Clark Ltd., Edinburgh

CONTENTS

Preface

The life and commitments of a Scottish minister of the present day are surely vividly enough known, with their endless demands on time, knowledge and study, personality, patience, and Christian dedication. But the Church in Scotland has evolved through recent centuries in somewhat tortuous and sometimes tempestuous fashion; and the day to day lives of both shepherds and their flocks, as they were even a century back, are shrouded in a mist of largely unstudied memories.

The object of this study is to draw together, from a wealth of diverse original sources, a clearer picture of what Scottish Church life meant to both minister and people through the long years between 1800 and the days of our immediate fathers. In so doing, we shall more fully understand what manner of heritage is ours; we shall see more clearly how the labours, the successes, and even the failures of our forefathers have contributed to the building of our present Church in Scotland; and we shall more readily appreciate Scotland's peculiar affection for its ministers which is in some measure the result of our nation's history and in some measure the cause of it.

Foreword

This is a book which tells of the life and work of the Scottish minister in the nineteenth century. Few periods of history are so ill known as those immediately preceding our own, too recent to be taught in the classroom and too distant to be remembered. The life of the Church is no exception to this. Many prejudices about the Scottish ministers of a bygone generation are often found, and a great deal of ignorance, but here is a picture drawn in great detail from a wide variety of sources. There is no attempt to conceal or excuse the limitations or eccentricities of these men, but the background to all is the faithful and devoted round of duty trodden by the average minister, his care for his people and his faithfulness in the Gospel.

No uniformity existed. There was a wide gap between the typical Moderate of the eighteenth century whose portrait was drawn by Alexander Carlyle of Inveresk and the Evangelical, the one genteel, cultured, and not over active, and the other passionate in his convictions and continually involved in the life of the community. From the first years of the nineteenth century the numbers and influence of the Evangelicals grew until 1843 saw the division of the Scottish Church and the formation of the Free Church. A contrast also existed between the men like Norman MacLeod of the Barony who ministered among the crowded streets and the grim tenements of the industrial communities and those who walked the country roads from farm to farm, and a further one between the average minister in Lowland Scotland and his Gaelic-speaking brother in the Highlands and Islands. All these contrasts – and others – are to be found in these pages. As he reads of men who lived and thought in ways often remote from those of today, the modern reader may often be critical, but it is worth noting that the evidence against the Scottish clergy is provided by themselves. They were their own sternest critics.

A minister's primary duties were the conduct of worship on the Lord's Day and the pastoral care of his people through the other days of the week. Sermons were often incredibly long and congregations were intolerant of ministers who read their sermons. Long hours of preparation and memorising in the study were therefore required. Sometimes, but by no means always, the result was a crowded church, and in an age when the media offered virtually no competition the 'popular preacher' in a central city charge was a well-known Victorian phenomenon.

But it was also expected that a minister would know his flock individually, and this meant constant visiting, and especially of the sick. At one time a minister's visitation was indeed a visitation in the other sense of the word, but as the century passed it took on a more social character for the most part. So full were a minister's days that family life, especially when there were children in the manse, could be neglected. Money was never too plentiful in manses. If a minister had an income greater than that of many of his people he also had endless responsibilities, but nowhere is the life of the Victorian minister more obviously different from that of his successor today, than in the expectation that, however short money might be, there would always be servants in the manse.

Beyond his primary duties, a minister was usually engaged in a wide range of public activities ranging from savings banks, parish libraries, and public bodies to Sundays Schools and Bible Classes, and meetings to foster causes such as Temperance. In addition the country minister of those days, instead of renting, commonly farmed his own glebe, the acres of land adjoining the manse which provided him with part of his income. And always of course, there was prayer, private devotion, and the daily reading of the Bible. It was a full and active life, and the centre of Christian devotion in hundreds of parishes throughout the length and breadth of Scotland. And he had, of course, though he may seem to have forgotten the fact in his busy days, a wife in the manse.

JAMES BULLOCH

CHAPTER 1

Six days shalt thou labour

For as long as the Christian Church has employed full-time professional clergymen, tongue-in-cheek critics have said that such beings rightly belong in the ranks of the under-employed, being apparently liable for only one day's work in each week. Any typical clergyman of today would, not unnaturally, protest that evidence to support such a slander, at least in the present day, could come only from the total 'outsider' casting the most casual of glances at the public duties of the lazy cleric. He would further expect a deafening chorus of support from his many perspiring colleagues, and he would earnestly hope that this same chorus would immediately reverberate round the halls of that great presbytery in the skies where sit the faithful fathers of our Scottish Kirk. But there are discordant voices in the choir.

Thomas Chalmers, for example, is rightly regarded as the supreme guiding genius of the Free Church, in its conception, its birth and its rapid growth. His labours for the Church of Christ were, said Sydney Smith, like those of a thousand men: Lord Cockburn hailed him as 'one of the four greatest Scotsmen of all time': two dynamic ministries in Glasgow did not allow for any idle moments. Yet in 1805, as the young parish minister of Kilmany in Fife, he had written a pamphlet which contained this sentence: 'The author can assert, from what is to him the highest of all authority, the authority of his own experience, that after the satisfactory discharge of his parish duties, a minister may enjoy five days in the week of uninterrupted leisure for the prosecution of any science in which his taste may dispose him to engage.' Chalmers did, however, put his own record straight in a speech to the General Assembly of 1825, in which he admitted that such opinions were uttered in ignorance and pride and were quite wrong. This episode might be dismissed as the hasty comment of an inexperienced clergyman finding himself bored with a small rural parish, and certainly the young

Chalmers was immediately taken to task by Cupar Presbytery for his dereliction of duty on such a wide and regular scale. There is, however, more to it.

The same year, 1805, that saw the Scottish Church take somewhat shocked note of the young man from Kilmany, marked the death of Alexander Carlyle who had been prominent in Church life for close on fifty years. Viewed in one way, this colourful minister of Inveresk might seem to present a picture of a parish minister more in keeping with present-day ideals. He had, for example, the vision and the courage to begin a Sunday School in his parish at a time (1790) when these organisations were still widely distrusted as 'nurseries of sedition': his epitaph in the country churchyard, from the pen of the philosopher, Adam Ferguson, records that 'he was faithful to his pastoral charge, to his people a willing guide in the ways of righteousness and truth': a further tribute, from Chief Commissioner Adam, states that 'he had nothing in him that detracted from or was unbecoming the character of a clergyman', while one of his successors at Inveresk found ample evidence that he had visited his people acceptably and that 'his interest in the poorest of his flock was noteworthy'. At national level, Carlyle was clearly held in high esteem, being elected Moderator of Synod and failing in his bid to become Clerk to the General Assembly only on a second vote.

Against this, however, in his autobiography Carlyle admits that his congregation in Inveresk were reluctant to receive him as their minister because of his known un-ministerial behaviour. He was, for instance, frequently absent from his parish for long spells indulging his taste for the gay social life of London; he confesses, without much sign of repentance, to 'philandering with the ladies', to consuming vast quantities of claret to the extent that he would shun any company where the supply of this or similar beverages might be inadequate – Presbytery dinners, for example, where the wine allowance was too paltry – and to revelling in such leisure pursuits as dancing, whist, billiards and theatre-going at a time when all of these were most definitely 'out-of-bounds' to clergymen.

With this in mind, Chalmers may have been speaking the truth when he affirmed at his Presbytery 'trial', 'I expend as much effort upon the religious improvement of my people as any minister within the bounds of my Presbytery.' Chalmers was not content, as apparently Carlyle was, to fritter away lengthy off-duty hours on the pleasures of the flesh. In fact, he worked very hard, teaching classes in Mathematics and Chemistry on a private basis for five days in each week in St. Andrews. Conversely, Carlyle may have been less than fair to himself in many ways. These individual cases are mentioned in an exemplary sense. A much more widespread review is needed if we are to see the normal daily life and work of the Scottish parish minister as the nineteenth century got into its stride.

Midway through the eighteenth century, the vast majority of the Church of Scotland's ministers were ranged in the two opposing and increasingly hostile camps of Moderates and Evangelicals, and each group became more and more intolerant of the other's interpretation of how the Christian ministry should be exercised. So bitter did the exchanges between them become that a simple reading of the one side's estimate of the other's clergy could only lead a stranger to give thanks to God that the Christian Church in Scotland was able to survive a period when so much of its parochial leadership was of such unworthy character.

Care is needed in sifting the evidence to differentiate between genuine neglect of essential duty and vindictive criticism of honest men whose only 'crime' was that they genuinely interpreted the functions of a minister in a different way. For example, it was said that the Moderates preferred the Arts to the Scriptures, were good shots but wretched preachers, spent more time with the sheep on the profitable glebe-farms than with the lost sheep among their parishioners; but many of these attacks stemmed really from the basic difference in the way the two sides saw the work of the ministry.

The Moderates believed, as William Neil says, 'that politics, literature, and the wide issues that affect men in all aspects of their environment are equally the concern of the ministry'; they regarded all knowledge and learning as worthy subjects for the involvement of the clergy. So their concept of the ministry was inevitably enlarged beyond the mere pastoral care of a parish, and in several outstanding cases the result was that the culture and learning of Scotland greatly benefited. Speaking in the General Assembly of 1791, the same Alexander Carlyle could quite truthfully say, 'There are few branches of literature in which the ministers of the Church have not excelled; there are few subjects of fine writing in which they do not stand foremost in the ranks of authors. We have men who have successfully enlightened the world in every branch. Who have written the best histories ancient and modern? It has been clergymen of this Church. Who has written the clearest delineation of the human understanding and all its powers? A clergyman of this Church. Who has written the best system of rhetoric and exemplified it by his own orations? A clergyman of this Church. Who wrote a tragedy that has been deemed perfect? A clergyman of this Church. Who was the most profound mathematician of the age he lived in? A clergyman of this Church. Who wrote the best treatise on agriculture . . . ?' These were no idle boasts and no mean tribute to Moderatism, even if the Evangelicals, fiercely intolerant of any but their own kind and regarding themselves as the sole possessors and purveyors of truth, flayed such ministers, accusing them of neglecting essential duty to the extent of being liable to the undiluted wrath of heaven.

At the same time, however, the Evangelicals produced awesome evidence of clerical inefficiency and indiscretion which make the misdemeanours of Chalmers and Carlyle seem trivial. Neil Douglas, for example, tells of one minister in Kintyre who in eight years never once visited or prayed with his sick parishioners. In an even more neglected state was the parish of Thurso which in the forty-year period up to 1797 had not one single diet of catechism.

In the present day, two of the main duties of any ordained parish minister are to preach the Word and to administer the Sacraments: these, indeed, have been the basic inescapable duties of all generations of Reformed clergy, and they were every bit as central last century as this. How well or ill did the average Moderate fulfil this part of his 'remit'? We should not immediately assume that there were many ministers like the one in the Highlands cited by the Evangelical war-horse, John Kennedy, Free Church minister in Dingwall, who declared of his victim that 'he invariably preached a borrowed sermon which he had read so often that he himself was half asleep in delivering it'. Equally, we ought not to generalise from the behaviour of the incredible minister of Duthil who, it is said, possessed only two sermons and whose attempts at variety lay solely in announcing different texts from time to time. If, on the other hand, such an allegation might seem to smack much more of partisan exaggeration than of strict historical accuracy, there is corroborating evidence from Dr. W. Hanna, the highly esteemed son-in-law and biographer of Chalmers, for he too speaks of a similarly limited preacher of the Moderate School. After he had systematically delivered the same handful of sermons over many years, several of his exasperated members approached the beadle – so often in Scotland it was to this officer that men turned in such delicate matters – to see if, failing a whole new sermon, the minister might be persuaded at least to furnish a new text from time to time. 'Next Sunday, to the astonishment of the audience, the minister gave out a text from which he had never before preached. Every Bible was opened at the place, and the listeners leant back in their pews in eager anticipation of the new sermon.' Alas, after the reading of the text, from the Book of Genesis, the all too familiar sermon on Nicodemus was delivered word for word as before. One thing is certain: neither preacher would have been of much assistance to the sermon syndicate operating in Caithness in the 1750s, where the enrolled members pledged that any new sermons they might occasionally write would at once be made available to their colleagues.

The historian A. J. Campbell came to the conclusion that 'many of the later Moderates had lost faith in the office of preaching and, having composed sermons to suffice for a year or two they were content to repeat them in rotation for the rest of their lives'. Remembering that no less a figure than Principal Hill of St. Andrews had sermons for but three years in his 'barrel', it is easier to understand the savage attacks launched by the fervent Evangelicals against the Moderate Pulpit.

Much more worrying, however, were the Evangelicals' accusations of intemperance, immorality, and thoroughly irreligious behaviour in the Moderates' off-duty hours. Here is Donald Sage, for example, speaking of some of the ministers in Aberdeen Synod: 'Such was their general character as a body – many of them were so openly profane – that they were known as the most ungodly men in their respective congregations; two of them especially were the faithful representatives of the genuine Moderates of that day – they stuck at nothing, sabbath desecration, profane swearing, drunkenness, or the most open contempt of God's truth and ordinances'. These are strong words even for an Evangelical: if such men were entrusted with preaching the Word of God week by week, it might almost be better that they stuck to a few proven sermons, especially if they had originated from more saintly minds. Nor is Sage a lone voice. John Kennedy is no more flattering of the Highland Moderates that he had encountered: 'They were pests to all who were in earnest about salvation, and they formed a medium between the Church and the world through which the profanity of the ungodly came in to desecrate the House of God.' On a further occasion, he dismissed them in these terms, 'The only maxim in their code of morals was that a minister may do what he likes if he continues in safe possession of his living.' That even this rock-bottom standard proved too demanding for some is seen in the comment made by Dr. Norman Macleod, father of the saint of the Barony, when he left Campbeltown for Campsie in 1812: 'The only persons in the whole district with whom I parted without any feelings of regret were the clergy; in the course of a very few years, four or five libels were successively on our Presbytery table; they ended in the deposition of three members of Presbytery, while the fourth was withdrawn as the accused was insane; two of the remaining members of Presbytery were deposed.' Even Alexander Carlyle, who knew well how to enjoy himself in worldly pleasure, commented on a colleague in Yester – 'How to eat and sleep and drink were his sole care'.

There are two 'giants' who in their own way merit passing mention. John Kennedy of Dingwall delights to tell of an unnamed minister in the north who at the drinking bouts 'was the last to slide off his chair', not because he was more abstemious than the rest, but because he was 'more seasoned'. In a class by himself, however, was the Rev. Roderick McKenzie, minister of Knockbain in the 1820s. His wide reputation as a man who could consume vast quantities of alcohol and still remain upright and in control of most of his faculties, was acknowledged when a public challenge was arranged with a notorious winebibber and glutton from England: the drinking commenced and the minister triumphed gloriously; 'the only symptom of inebriety which he ever showed on this or any other occasion was to speak somewhat thick and to snivel through his nose'.

What of the Evangelicals who were so adamant that their Moderate brethren were unworthy examples to their flocks? In terms of numbers, the Evangelicals were very much in the minority until around 1800, and in fact it was only in the 1830s that their numerical strength equalled and on occasion began to surpass the Moderates in the General Assembly. Their voice, however, was always the louder: their criticism of their brother ministers was always the fiercer. The Moderates were not so given to launching vitriolic attacks on their opponents, with the result that direct comparison is difficult.

It would be comforting if the Moderates were restrained in their comments because of lack of ammunition, but the life of such a leading Evangelical as Alexander Webster raises doubts. He was, we are reliably told, 'a prince among the Evangelicals', and was minister from 1737 to 1784 of the Tolbooth Church in Edinburgh – 'the best attended Church in the town' – which was generally regarded by the Evangelicals as their 'Chief Citadel'. He had there a congregation that was 'devoted to him', he inaugurated the fund for widows and orphans of ministers, and he had a considerable share in the planning of Edinburgh's new town. Furthermore, he stood out boldly as a staunch guardian of his congregation's moral and spiritual welfare by warning them not to attend his church when Alexander Carlyle preached there – this because of Carlyle's active support of the commercial theatre. Like the same Carlyle, however, Webster was rather a man of two sides. He was, for instance, 'held to be excellent company even by those of dissolute manners, while being a five bottle man, he could lay them all under the table'. For Dr. Bonum Magnum, as he was rather fittingly nicknamed, 'aptness to pray was as easy and natural as to drink a convivial glass'.

The Moderates were in many instances less than inspiring; the Evangelicals scarcely seem more attractive if Webster could at any time be one of their leaders; one might easily conclude that the daily life, discipline and conduct of the Scottish minister at the outset of the nineteenth century was little short of scandalous. Clearly a counter-weight, if it can honestly be found, is needed to reassure us that God's work in Scotland was not being widely neglected by those whose full-time responsibility it was. Further evidence is happily available from two sources – the verdicts of some of the leading historians and commentators, and the accounts of two Churchmen who would have been leaders in any generation and who served the Church of our fathers faithfully and well in the last thirty years of the eighteenth century. The one was a staunch Moderate, the other an unrepentant Evangelical; yet, for more than twenty-five years, as colleagues in the same Church ministering to the same congregation, they worked happily and very productively side by side.

First, the historians. J. H. Millar assesses the clergy in his *Literary History of Scotland*: 'Never before or since have Scotland's ministers been so learned and at the same time so free from the patois of pedantry or puritanism. The Moderates defended the right of ministers to live like normal human kind instead of being at the mercy of the canting humbugs who identified their prejudices with Presbyterianism.' Nor is this enthusiastic appraisal unsupported: John Cunningham maintains that while the Moderates 'had no rules to hinder them from doing as other Christians did, yet they were with few exceptions men of exemplary lives': J. C. Fyfe, in a passage from his *Scottish Diaries and Memoirs*, comes firmly to the defence of Alexander Carlyle as a man who could 'keep his humanity and his joy of life and at the same time be a good Christian and a worthy minister of the Gospel'. It is always easy to echo the sentiments of Sir Roger de Coverley and say that 'much might be said on both sides'; in the present instance, however, this would appear to be the verdict, rightly arrived at, by the historians. A. J. Campbell, in general terms, finds both 'sides' largely innocent of the charges the one brought against the other: 'It is no longer possible to believe that the level of spiritual life was higher in one party or type than its rival. Throughout the country the standard of duty maintained by the parochial clergy was as excellent as at any other period. The Moderate was not a man of pagan mind and elastic morals, indifferent to the work of the ministry and addicted to the pleasures of the table. The average minister did his work faithfully according to the methods of the day. Preaching, catechising, visiting the sick, taking oversight of the parish school, and administering the poor relief of the parish

– in such matters there was no difference between the Moderate and the Evangelical.' To the list of ministerial duties we will in detail return.

Now it is the turn of those two men alluded to above who, while sitting on 'opposing front benches' in the General Assembly, yet combined most effectively in the parish of Old Greyfriars, Edinburgh. Senior of the two was William Robertson, whose father had become minister of that Church in 1733. After gaining valuable experience in the parish of Gladsmuir, East Lothian, and then in Lady Yester's, Edinburgh, the young Robertson was called to his father's pulpit in 1761. In him, says Professor Burleigh, 'the ideal of Moderatism was realised'. He was a historian fit to be talked of in the same breath as Voltaire, Hume and Gibbon; he was, from 1762 until 1780, the undisputed leader of the Moderate Party, which of course was the majority party in the Assembly; and he was until his death what Campbell calls 'the model parish minister'. In addition, he was the distinguished Principal of Edinburgh University.

It came, therefore, as a very considerable surprise when in 1767 he received as his colleague the Evangelical John Erskine, but a potentially explosive situation with the yoking of these two men who, theologically and ecclesiastically, were opposites, in practice proved to be a thoroughly amicable partnership. It showed that a good Moderate and a good Evangelical were both faithful servants of God and the Church in their respective ways, and that party considerations could take a poor second place to the main duties confronting a Scottish minister of the period.

Erskine had served in three parishes between his ordination and his call to Old Greyfriars – Kirkintilloch, Culross, and New Greyfriars – and his duties appear to have been largely the same in them all. His biographer, Sir Henry Moncreiff Wellwood of St. Cuthbert's, records that each Sunday he had to deliver three discourses (two sermons and a lecture), while his week-days were spent in the catechising of his people (each household had to be visited, questioned, and exhorted at least once a year), in visiting the sick and dying, in administering the poor fund, and in taking an active share in the running of the various charitable bodies. In short, Erskine did faithfully week by week all that

A. J. Campbell outlined as the duties of the normal parish minister, so that the picture we have of him is quite unlike the picture painted either by the young Chalmers or by Carlyle. Even without the work of Presbytery, even without added voluntary labours, Erskine and his conscientious colleagues were busy enough to refute any suggestion that the parish ministry might at this time be seen by any as part-time employment only.

It is to be hoped that the people of Old Greyfriars fully appreciated their uncommon good fortune in having two such stalwarts to lead them. Robertson, in one critic's estimation, was more than faithful to his many parochial duties: Erskine's biographer is in no doubt that his colleague was similarly conscientious: 'During the whole course of his ministry, Erskine served to make every part of his conduct, of his personal habits, of his time, of his public activity, and of his literary pursuits, to bear directly and constantly on his public or professional usefulness, in the service of the Gospel, as the great object of his life. . . . In the private exercise of his pastoral functions, he was as indefatigable among the lowest of the people entrusted to him, and in the minutest services which he could render them, as in the most conspicuous efforts of his literature and talents.'

Scotland's clergy cannot be exalted en masse on the strength of two dedicated men. The differences between the Moderates and the Evangelicals, and the weaknesses of a few undesirables in both camps cannot be ignored. As a group, the Moderates may well have paid less attention to theology in general and to preaching in particular than they should; they may on occasion have swung too far towards a secular approach to life in their desire to integrate the Church and the Arts; the Moderate leadership were perhaps over anxious to hush up blatant cases of clerical delinquency; but there were sufficient men of a like mind with Robertson to justify the confidence the historians feel as they review the overall state of the party. Likewise, the Evangelicals probably contained more than a healthy share of intolerance within their ranks; some of their number could be held to be illiberal and almost illiterate; there were traces of hypocrisy; but their overall concerns were right and rightly expressed. On the whole, Scotland's clergy, at the dawn of the nineteenth century, were not underworked in terms of what was expected of them, nor did many of them spare themselves in an attempt to do faithfully their duty.

At the same time, however, before we trace the changes that the century was to bring to Scottish ministers in terms of the life they lived and the work they were expected to do, we must note two further factors which must have had an effect on the concept of the parish ministry as the century opened. First, there was the continuing practice, exemplified in William Robertson, whereby a minister, in charge possibly of a large and demanding parish, could at the same time hold an appointment within a neighbouring university. At first glance, this could appear to be some kind of official 'recognition' that the 'statutory' duties of even a large parish were either insufficient to occupy an energetic man full-time (and that perhaps the young Chalmers was after all not so far wrong), or that they were not deemed so all-important relative to what a gifted clergyman might be able to contribute in specialist fields of education. Second, the kind of training divinity students were receiving in the Colleges is also relevant.

The whole business of pluralities is strange to modern ears. For example, when Robert Burns of Paisley entered Edinburgh University Divinity Faculty in 1805, he found all three Professors drawing stipends as parish ministers. Dr. Andrew Hunter had to divide his attentions between a class of up to 200 trainee ministers and his 'somewhat rugged metropolitan parish': Dr. Hugh Meiklejohn had a rather smaller parish (Abercorn), but it was fourteen miles distant from the University, and this at a time when travel and communications were far from easy. Little better was Dr. Ferrie who, from 1813, was both Professor of Civil History in St. Andrews and minister of Kilconquhar some twelve miles away. As late as 1824, despite commendable opposition from both Presbytery and Synod, Dr. Macfarlane was confirmed as minister of Glasgow, St. Mungo's – the foremost city Church – and as Principal of Glasgow University. In the city of Aberdeen in the same period, the minister of the important West Church was also a University Professor. In him, if we accept the verdict of W. G. Blaikie, all that was potentially dangerous in the system of pluralities was seen in reality, at least so far as this man's congregation was concerned: 'He did absolutely nothing for his flock beyond repeating his stereotyped prayers every Sunday morning and reading a drowsy discourse.' But, even if there had been no pluralists guilty of neglecting either their flock or their students, it would still be difficult to commend the practice. There would always be the temptation for men holding such double appointments increasingly to forsake the mundane and often trying problems of a parish in favour of the more stimulating atmosphere of a University or College: if future ministers were trained by pluralists, they could perhaps deduce, even subconsciously, that the parishes awaiting them would not be too demanding on their time and that they in turn could seek extra-parochial employment.

The crucial question is how demanding in terms of time the inescapable duties of a parish minister were, and on this there is much to be said for the sentiments of Stevenson MacGill, minister of Glasgow's Tron Church from 1797, and of Andrew Thomson, inducted as first minister of St. George's, Edinburgh, in 1814. As opposition to the whole practice of pluralities gathered momentum with voices raised from pulpit and pew, from individuals and Church Courts, these two men put into words what many were by that time thinking. Said MacGill, who had already declined a plurality involving a parish and a Professorship in St. Andrews, 'I appeal to the experience of my brethren of this city of Glasgow, to the most faithful and diligent, and I would ask them if they have been able to discharge their duties with satisfaction, if many most important duties they have not been forced to neglect, if they have not often felt their spirits sink into despondency at the thought of how little they have done for their people.' On another occasion he was even more pointed: 'unions of offices always had a very pernicious effect on both sides'. No less forceful was Thomson: in a speech to the Assembly, he affirmed, 'I could no more perform what is justly expected of a Professor along with my labours as a parish minister than I could fly to the moon.' This sentiment was expressed somewhat more colloquially by a spokesman for the vacant parish of Colinton in the capital city. Being offered a Dr. Walker whom they cared little for, their opposition was rendered total when it was explained, as an alleged attraction, that he would very likely be appointed a Professor in the University: 'That makes the thing far waur; he will just mak' a bye job of our souls.'

The days of pluralities were numbered, and their fate was finally sealed, first by an Act of Assembly in 1817 forbidding pluralities unless the minister's parish was in or near the University town, and then by a report of the Royal Commission on the Universities in 1828 which stated that pluralities were 'inexpedient'. So the necessary legislation was introduced; hitherto, the only relevant deliverances of Assembly had been designed to prohibit a minister becoming too immersed in certain secular affairs. He was not allowed, for example, to be a Member of Parliament, a senator of the College of Justice, a tavern keeper or a major-domo; he could, however, be factor of an estate or head of an Academy or, as we shall have cause to note later, a medical practitioner. In fairness, however, it was not either greed on the part of ministers or lack of normal parish work that prolonged the existence of pluralities. Scottish universities at this time could not afford to pay adequate living salaries to their staff, while in the eighteenth century the ministers formed easily the most learned class in society, so that universities looked naturally to them to fill Professorial posts, not only in the Faculty of Divinity but in other Faculties as well. This situation posed many problems for the conscientious minister who, called to a University appointment, might dearly have wished to accept but could not do so economically without operating a personally unsatisfactory plurality. However 'inexpedient' the system of pluralities may have been, there was some justification for it at the time, and it surely gives us cause for pride in this regard, that our clerical forefathers were academically of such a high calibre.

Turning now to the training divinity students were receiving at the end of the eighteenth and the beginning of the nineteenth centuries, there are really three main points to be considered, viz.: the standard of University education as a whole, the standard of teaching in the Divinity Faculties, and the syllabus of studies provided.

The most striking feature in the average university class of this period was the extreme youth of many of the students, who in the present day would only be at the stage of leaving Primary School. For instance, among the distinguished ministers who began their university courses when only twelve years of age were Thomas Guthrie, Robert Candlish, James Begg and Alexander Moody Stuart, all of whom entered University between 1815 and 1821. Thomas Chalmers had gone one better by enrolling in St. Andrews University in 1791 when he was only eleven, while in 1768, Glasgow College had witnessed the arrival of a truly precocious child in the person of John Jamieson, aged nine. The same Jamieson, later a distinguished minister of the Secession Church in Forfar and in Edinburgh, went on to that denomination's college in Alloa when only fourteen. With some of these early entrants there was certainly academic ability well above the average – Jamieson apparently could read the New Testament at the age of four – but with many others, ability was little more than average, with the result that university studies in many subjects could not be of a very advanced nature. In particular, it was found extremely difficult to teach philosophy in any depth to students who were still virtually children. In truth, universities were much more like upper High Schools than anything which today would readily be termed a 'university'.

There was no entrance examination, and no minimum academic qualifications were laid down for entry; and further, once in the university, the students were encouraged neither to specialise nor to sit degree examinations and graduate. In St. Andrews University in the late 1830s, a certain student presented himself for his Latin degree exam only to be met by the janitor with the news that he had passed. He was naturally puzzled that he had passed an examination which he had not yet sat, but the janitor was adamant that his good tidings came from the Professor himself, adding, not entirely as an afterthought, 'The Professor is off to the fishing.'

Within the Divinity Faculties, there is a rather alarming mass of evidence that suggests that, not only were the students of too tender an age and perhaps little better in prior education than schoolboys, but that the Professors were hardly of a calibre to bring out the best in them. Admittedly, students never have been easily convinced of their Professors' abilities: a would-be minister is a harsher critic than most when surveying the senior members of the fraternity, and the Professors were by and large of the Moderate school and therefore could scarcely hope to impress any determined Evangelical. This said, however, there are some disturbing allegations. Alexander Carlyle, around 1740, dismissed the Professor of Divinity in Edinburgh as 'Dull, Dutch, and prolix'; George Cook, a leading Moderate before and after the Disruption, said of St. Andrews, 'The chairs were regarded as retreats for men who had nearly exhausted their energy in the ministerial office, who had passed the period of life during which new plans of intellectual effort are formed, and who rested satisfied with dwelling upon some of the common-place topics of theology.' This is bad enough, but, if Donald Sage is to be taken at his word, things in Aberdeen were worse. Speaking in general terms of the University as he found it early in the nineteenth century, he says, 'My attendance at the Aberdeen Hall was of no benefit to me whatsoever; I knew nothing at all of theology or the Bible, nor was I made to know anything of them by my public teachers.' Singled out for special mention was Dr. William Laurence Brown, who somehow tried to combine posts as Principal of Marischal College, Professor of Divinity, teacher of elocution, and minister of Greyfriars Church: 'I never heard him pronounce even once in his lectures during my four years' attendance at the Hall the name of Jesus Christ.'

These must have been dark days in our northern University, and lengthy ones too according to the comments of W. G. Blaikie, who was a student in Marischal College in the 1830s: 'Some of the Professors were of superior attainments, others deficient in the art of teaching, and one knew hardly anything of the proper subject of his chair. There was nothing in our Divinity Hall to make our studies attractive and there was no theological enthusiasm among us.' The fourth University, that at Glasgow, though praised highly by Carlyle mid-way through the eighteenth century, seems to have fallen victim to the same staffing weaknesses: the biographer of James Hamilton, minister of Regent Square Church, London, is less than flattering of its theological teaching in the 1830s: 'In some theological classes a beneficial influence was exerted on the student, but in others, if the young men did not educate themselves, they fared the worse. In some cases patronage had filled a chair in accordance with some obscure private connections, in flagrant defiance alike of the public opinion and the public good. A person endued with a perennial childishness not very many degrees above absolute imbecility, might, if he gained the patron's favour, be placed in a chair in which he should doze and vegetate for half a century to the unspeakable injury of two generations.' Thus patronage, so distasteful to so many congregations, afflicted the colleges: and not only in this way, because many of the all too rare bursaries for students were in the hands of patrons who disbursed them according to personal whim and not in accordance with need or ability.

The most worrying feature of the university training provided for divinity students, however, was that until well through the nineteenth century, there was little attempt made at practical training. What we would regard as Practical Theology was not listed among the subjects covered, even inadequately, by the professors charged with the education of the ministry, so that Norman Maclean, in his *Life of Cameron Lees of St. Giles*, can say, 'At that time there was no practical training given in the Divinity Halls, and students were licensed to preach having been taught everything except how to preach and how to set about their work as ministers.' It was not until 1872 that the first lecturers in practical theology were appointed, and even then there were only two to cover the four universities. Even as late as 1896, John Macleod of Govan felt justified in saying, 'The truth is that at present, strictly speaking, the Church provides no *ministerial* training; that is to say, the training which she accepts may be merely academic, and it is provided, not by her but by the Universities.'

Macleod himself did considerable pioneering work in this direction in Govan and would have done much more had he not died in 1898 when only fifty-eight years of age. Cameron Lees, too, did what he could by inviting the Edinburgh students to come to the Moray Aisle in St. Giles' Cathedral each week for lectures in practical matters, but right to the end of the nineteenth century, divinity students, though more fortunate than their colleagues of a hundred years earlier, were greatly deficient in preparation for the daily routine of administering a parish. As we think of newly ordained men in 1800, our sympathies are with them and their congregations, and we cannot but marvel that such one-sided training yet produced so many fine preachers and pastors. At this date in Scotland, even adequate pulpit experience was not afforded to students, as they were not allowed to undertake pulpit supply, which students today find such a valuable training ground. As Thomas Smith remarks in his biography of James Begg, 'In Begg's time [he was a student in the 1820s] I believe that a student preaching without licence would have been regarded as guilty of something of the nature of ecclesiastical insubordination.'

Divinity training could be both defective and deficient, but a peculiarity of the times, happily unknown today, could, in the early years of the nineteenth century, effectively nullify such sound teaching as there was. Until 1827, when one term's actual attendance at a Divinity Hall was made a necessary precondition in one seeking to be licensed, divinity students were permitted to go forward to that stage without having attended any classes in the Faculty of Divinity. Prior to that, the Church recognised what it euphemistically called 'partial attendance' at such Halls over a period of six sessions. Just how partial this could be is seen in the report issued in 1830 by the Royal Commission of Inquiry into the state of the Universities in Scotland: 'The Church recognises what is termed irregular attendance which is in fact no attendance whatever.' Two hard examples illustrate the literal truth of this. Patrick Brewster was licensed by the Presbytery of Fordoun in 1817 after five incomplete sessions in Edinburgh and one incomplete session in Aberdeen. His idea of 'incomplete' involved attendance at one meeting in each session. In a similar vein, Dr. Andrew Thomson of St. George's, Edinburgh, said in 1826: 'I know a gentleman, who is now a minister of the Church, who taught a school in the country; he came at the beginning of a session, enrolled, paid his fee, got his ticket, walked home and taught his school the whole winter. Then he came back and got his certificate of regular attendance.' In passing, it is worth noting that Donald Sage who, as we saw, criticised Dr. Brown most severely, attended only two sessions of that Professor's lectures with anything like regularity, although the course took six sessions to complete. It may be that many a professor's reputation suffered unjustly at the hands of students who could scarcely judge on first-hand knowledge.

On reflection, there are several unsatisfactory aspects – Presbyteries whose supervision of their divinity students was an empty formality; the national Church apparently unconcerned for the proper training of its future leaders; and the questionable sense of dedication shown by the students themselves. But, as with the system of pluralities, there may be some justification for permitting some scheme of partial attendance. Bursaries were few and fees were not small, so that many students could not afford full-time study on a regular basis. The parochial school system in Scotland depended on divinity students for staffing and the whole system would have collapsed overnight if full-time attendance at divinity hall had been insisted on. To this extent, the Church could be said to be safeguarding the general education of the country at the sacrificial expense of its own professional education; but it was a system of training that had to be superseded by compulsory university attendance on something like our present pattern.

What, then, do we say thus far of the ministers of our land at the beginning of the nineteenth century? Leaving to one side both our pride that the Universities recognised them as the intellectual cream of their former students, and our disappointment that the behaviour of a few was manifestly not what it ought to have been, we can surely rest satisfied that on the whole the vast majority of these men were quietly doing God's daily work to the best of their ability. Improvements there could be; changes there would have to be; but as Scotland entered the nineteenth century, the average minister was, in terms of the age in which he lived, a well-educated man, a busy man, and a conscientious and faithful servant of his God.

CHAPTER 2

Go ye into all the world and preach the Gospel

It is quite possible for a parish minister to be well-educated, industrious, and conscientious, and yet rouse little response from his parishioners as a whole. For example, in today's vast new housing areas despite many years of Herculean labours, the faithful minister can still see only a few hundred souls out of many thousands whose lives are, with any regularity, within the orbit of the Church. We turn now to an assessment of how far the average minister of the nineteenth century attempted to be minister of his parish as well as of his congregation, and of the Scottish people's willingness to be influenced by him, with special attention to any changes that the century brought in this regard as life in Scotland took on 'a more modern look' and as the ministers' interpretation of their parochial responsibilities altered.

There were during the nineteenth century two quite different 'Scotlands'. There was the vast majority of the country, geographically speaking, which was still largely rural and where the way of life and the size and make-up of the population was slow to alter; and there were the industrial areas, centred mainly on Glasgow and Edinburgh, where, throughout the century, the arrival of thousands of immigrants from the country areas created enormous social problems of overcrowding, poverty and disease. The task facing a minister in such circumstances was quite unlike that which his brother minister had to contend with elsewhere in Scotland. His particular parochial problems will be examined as a separate item.

For much of the nineteenth century, our present-day framework of week-night organisations within the Church Hall was totally unknown – the Boys' Brigade, for example, was not born until 1883, while the Woman's Guild was a further three years behind. Furthermore, there was not the same pressure then as now in regular fund-raising to maintain the Churches – in the vast majority of the congregations, money received from endowments and from the local heritors was sufficient to meet normal requirements. It was not until the Free Church, newly established as a result of the Disruption in 1843, was faced with the burden of paying its ministers and school-teachers, and, at the same time, of erecting new buildings, that ordinary worshippers in Scotland in any large numbers were asked either to dig deeply and regularly into their own pockets, or to devise means of persuading non-Churchgoers to part with their money in the Church's cause. This being so, the Church lacked, at the outset of the nineteenth century, some of the 'weapons' which, in our own day, have proved highly successful in involving the parishioners, as distinct from the members of the congregations, in her work.

In short, she depended almost solely on the desire of the people to join in purely religious activities. First and foremost this meant that the Church had to depend on the Sunday services drawing the people, although these, early in the nineteenth century, were increasingly supplemented by week-night classes and lectures, always serious in tone, usually Biblical in theme, and almost invariably conducted by the local minister. Now, thinking of our present position in which it is extremley difficult to persuade the majority of our people to listen to the Church's message when it is undiluted and unadorned by some of the more secular trimmings of modern Church life, it might appear that, as things were at the beginning of the nineteenth century, any widespread popular interest in the Church must reflect credit both on our Scottish ancestors as being inherently devout, and on the ministers as being dynamic and efficient.

It would be churlish to deny the clergy credit in this direction, and there are certain facts and figures that might indicate a genuine piety on the part of many ordinary folk: in the meantime, however, we must be aware of certain elements in Scottish life at the beginning of the nineteenth century which, absent today, did help to foster an atmosphere in which the minister's task was made easier, and in which it was more difficult for a man to drift uninterestedly away from the Church. (Things in the large towns could be substantially different.)

To begin with, the parish minister still claimed, as his right, entry into every home in his parish at least once a year to attend to the catechising of the children and the servants: as we shall see, the tenor of these visits would help to keep many on the straight and narrow path. The Kirk Sessions, too, though lacking their near-dictatorial powers of a century before, still carried considerable weight in a community, and it was a serious business to fall foul of them. Not unimportant was the fact that the Church disbursed the money in the Poor Fund until 1845 and controlled the Schools until 1872: as Stewart Mechie so rightly comments, 'So long as the Church retained its control of the poor-relief system and of education, it could not be ignored by any citizen, not even by those who rejected its teaching and separated themselves from its worship and fellowship. Nowadays its influence is so indirect that masses of the population can ignore it.' As telling a factor as any, however, was the strength of the Church's overall influence which ensured that, on the Lord's Day, even the openly profane could find little to be engaged in unless in the business of the Lord. Family prayers each night were still the rule rather than the exception, so it is not surprising that the average country minister could find as did John Macdonald on his introduction to Ferintosh in 1813, 'with very few exceptions all the parishioners attend the Church'. Similarly Henry Duncan, in so many ways a model parish minister, was able to serve all his 1,100 parishioners in Ruthwell, Dumfriesshire, without losing touch with even one family. By the same token, Professor W. Garden Blaikie of the Chair of Apologetics and Pastoral Theology in New College affirms, 'The time was when a simple announcement of the intention to open a Bible Class would be sure to draw together the chief part of those whose presence was desired.'

Of this last fact, we might note just two outstanding examples. The Rev. Andrew Somerville, in later years the first foreign mission secretary of the U.P. Church, instituted a series of lectures, some weekly, some monthly, while minister of Dumbarton from 1830 to 1845. He lectured once a month on Daniel, taking, it seems, two and a half years to arrive at the eleventh chapter, but far from either the topic or the rate of progress proving tedious, these lectures 'excited much interest' and 'effectually aroused Dumbarton'. The same man lectured weekly to crowds of one hundred and twenty on such subjects as 'effectual calling', 'justification', 'adoption', and 'sanctification'. These could hardly have been light discourses: likewise his sixteen lectures on 'the Mosaic dispensation as it was set up at Sinai' were intellectually demanding to a formidable degree: yet here again he can report that he found no lack of attention in his many hearers; rather, he says, they were 'unusually rivetted'. Not even the knowledge that he concluded each lecture with a searching series of questions could diminish the attendance.

Similar scenes were witnessed in the Ayrshire parish of Loudoun in the five years before the Disruption as large crowds of the local weavers filled every available seat at the parish minister's weekly lectures on Geology. The first such series drew attendances of one hundred and fifty, with as many locked outside the already over-crowded building: finding more spacious accommodation and even greater public interest, the second series boasted attendances of between six and seven hundred. The same thing was being repeated in many other parts of Scotland: in Rosneath, for example, the elder Story lectured to capacity audiences; in Ellon, the young Professor Robertson was similarly successful, while in Arbirlot Thomas Guthrie had an acute accommodation problem for any lecture he gave. This was, accordingly, a period when our forefathers were, by a combination of nature and circumstance, inclined to take an active interest in whatever the Church might do or organise. Some of their reasons may have been selfish; the lack of feasible alternative occupations for their leisure time would also contribute, but in the early part of the nineteenth century a popular concern for the Church and its message was more genuinely widespread than anything we witness today.

Such popular interest, however, was not to continue through the whole century. Professor Blaikie traces the crucial change in public attitude to the 1870s on the grounds that, by that time, the parish minister had lost that measure of public authority and private influence which had been able to command automatic attention. The younger Story's experiences in Rosneath both confirm and, partially at least, explain this. He succeeded his father in this parish in 1859 and specifically records that one of the main changes that took place was that, despite repeated strenuous efforts, interest in the mid-week lectures, so well attended in the forty years of his father's ministry, dwindled alarmingly. The decline, he says, was particularly marked in the

1870s, and he attributes this to the advent of the penny papers and cheap magazines, and to the rapid development of the railways. In other words, the ordinary folk of Scotland were by this time being given more opportunity to think for themselves by being able to read views and opinions other than those presented from the pulpit. Travel was opening up new horizons to them and introducing them to the differing ways both of the English and of the continentals. The civil authorities had taken from the Church control of education and certain important aspects of social welfare, with the result that the local Church and its minister did not appear so omnipotent and omniscient as in former days.

One way or another, the average Scot was feeling more independent, more inclined to question and less disposed to abide quietly by tradition. Those willing to study had access to the new philosophies, many of which were at odds with the doctrines of the Kirk. Hegelianism, for example, 'stirred currents of thought in Scotland which were sapping both the philosophy of "common sense" and the theology of Calvinism'. Those not academically inclined were less willing to endure week by week the outpourings of the pulpit simply because Sunday offered little alternative. Cameron Lees of St. Giles' Cathedral is refreshingly honest about this in a letter he wrote to Charteris in 1907: 'The people, the young men in particular, are neglecting the Church because they find it a bore.' In support, Lees quotes parents who, God-fearing themselves, could not persuade their sons to go near a Church. He tells of preaching to a crowd of 1,000, almost all of whom were women; and he predicts that Sunday would more and more become a day of open amusement with the young folk providing their own cures for their Sabbath boredom. Principal Story was even more pessimistic as the nineteenth century ended; no longer, as it seemed to him, was it a question of apathy or boredom that kept people from Church; nor was it that the people were having philosophical doubts about certain aspects of religion; rather he felt that many had made up their minds and come to a conclusion that was at total variance with the Church's central creed. Writing a tribute to Mrs. Oliphant in 1897, he says, 'in these days, agnosticism seems to be thought a kind of distinction even in women'.

With the approach of the twentieth century, the Church and its ordained servants, faced, even in the remoter country areas, a noticeably harder task in gaining the ear of their parishioners at large. The Church was having to adapt itself to meet the changing situation – the blossoming of something akin to our modern-day pattern of organisations was just one development, and to this we shall return – and its ministers were having, more than formerly, to present their message in both a reasoned and an attractive way. Their audiences, which a hundred years before had been almost automatically in their places before them, now had to be won.

So far the emphasis has been on the mid-week classes rather than on the Sunday services. We did note, certainly, that Macdonald in Ferintosh had no complaints on the attendance of his parishioners at Church. Norman Macleod, too, found that his Church on a Sunday was no less crowded than was his lecture-room: 'The Church was regularly crowded to suffocation with both stairs and passages occupied.' In Kilmany, such were the crowds, both of parishioners and of visiting strangers, who were anxious to hear the preaching of the 'new' and 'Evangelical' Thomas Chalmers that the windows of the Church were removed to allow those who had to stand outside in the churchyard a chance to hear. For all that, however, Sunday attendances in the country areas saw the same general decline towards the end of the century as was noted in connection with the lectures, and for more or less the same reasons.

One religious festival in the country districts brought the whole parish to the Church more successfully than anything else ever did. During that period when the celebration of the Lord's Supper was regarded as the high-spot on both the religious and the social calendar, a minister really had the chance to 'get to grips' with his parishioners for as long as five days at a stretch. The accepted pattern was that the Sacrament should be celebrated just once each year in each parish, generally in the summer months as much of the ceremony was enacted out of doors, usually in the Churchyard. The 'rationing' of the sacramental occasions did not, however, mean that the Church members had to go without the Sacrament for the other fifty-one weeks of the year. On a parish's communion Sunday, the neighbouring ministers converged to lend support to their colleague; their own churches were therefore closed, but such was the appeal of the Sacramental occasion, and of the festivities associated with it, that many of their people journeyed with them, with the result that the more determined could contrive to be at some communion service almost every Sunday in the summer. There were those who would cheerfully walk ten or more miles just to be present at the Sacrament; Norman Macleod's *Reminiscences of a Highland Parish* has this fairly typical example: 'Old John Cameron, with fourscore-years-and-ten to carry, had walked from Kinloch, ten miles across pathless hills. Other patriarchs, with staff in hand, had come greater distances.'

Understandably, the crowds present at a Communion could be enormous and quite out of proportion to the Church's normal membership. At Grandtully in Perthshire, 5,000 attended Communion in 1841 and 'hardly an individual moved' in the five hours that the main service lasted. At one Communion in Uig in Lewis, the crowd was put at 9,000, and A. J. Campbell cites records of as many as 10,000 attending in a parish where the normal population the rest of the year totalled only 1,000. Wherever possible, a famous preacher was included among the ministerial guests officiating, and this naturally served to accentuate further the problems of crowd control. In Aberdeen Gaelic Chapel, for instance, John Macdonald of Ferintosh, the Apostle of the North, was the regular guest preacher at the Communion Season for close on twenty years, and on each occasion the Church was so crowded that he had to find his way to the pulpit by climbing over the backs of the pews.

Thus, the parish minister was annually presented with a golden opportunity of impressing his people with the relevance of the Gospel. Rightly handled, such occasions could have made a profound impact on many lives, always provided that the mood throughout was reverent and the conduct of both clergy and people seemly. Certainly there is abundant evidence to suggest that the clergymen did not spare themselves physically. Writing of his father's ministry, the younger Story describes in graphic detail what the Communion Season could be like in the early part of the nineteenth century: 'It was a point of honour, in which each parish tried to rival its neighbour, that the Communion Services should be prolonged as much as possible, and it was by no means rare that, beginning at 11 a.m., they should drag their slow length along till 6 or 7 in the evening. While the Communicants were receiving the Sacrament at successive tables in the Church, the people outside clustered round the "tent" in the Churchyard and listened to protracted preachings, one minister rising as soon as another sat down exhausted with as dauntless a devotion as that of Knight or Squire in the "desperate ring" at Flodden.'

The 'tent' was an erection looking like a cross between a bathing hut and a sentry box which afforded some protection from the elements for the officiating ministers, and, to a degree, assisted in projecting the voice of the preacher. It was well used because despite the vast crowds attending at Communion time, the actual numbers taking the bread and wine were normally very small. In the preliminary preaching which preceded the actual Sacrament, the Table was 'fenced', with those present being warned of the sin of going to the Table if their lives and conduct were unworthy. In the Highlands, particularly, this was so rigorously applied that the Sacrament came to be regarded, by clergy and people, not as a means of grace but as a 'mark of high spiritual attainment'. So high could the 'fence' be in certain places that Norman Maclean comments, 'The success of a preacher of the Gospel was judged not by the number he brought to the Holy Table, but by the number whose consciences were so touched that they had not the heart to come forward.' To those who judged by such standards, Roderick Macleod, inducted to Bracadale in 1823, must have been almost a saint inasmuch as, out of a population of 1,800, almost all of whom were present at the Communion celebrations, only 8 went forward to the table. Incidentally, his views on baptism were similarly strict and appeal was made to the Presbytery as the number of unbaptised children in the parish soared. This case dragged on for twenty years, but it did not prevent him becoming Moderator of the Free Church Assembly.

At the same time as this Macleod was resolutely 'fencing' the table in Skye, another of the clan – Alexander – was similarly efficient in Uig in Lewis. He was so shocked at the 'deplorable spiritual ignorance of his people' that it was not until his third year in the parish that he felt able to hold the Sacrament. Even then there were only five 'worthy' souls and 'at them the vast congregation looked on in dumb amazement'. Neither Macleod, however, was the equal of the incumbent of Duirinish where, from 1829 to 1840, communion was totally withheld on the grounds that there were no parishioners worthy of it. One parishioner is on record as saying, 'If you had asked me to commit the greatest sin, you could not have frightened me half so much as by inviting me to sit at the Table of the Lord.'

In parts of the north, too, the 'fence' was further reinforced by the supervisory activities of 'The Men'. Sprung from the peasantry, these were austere, rigid, fanatical laymen who were venerated for their Godliness and who asserted power over minister and people alike. Under their spiritual tyranny, all poetry and music, all the arts and fancies of the Highland mind, were banished as unclean. They organised Sunday night meetings in the homes of the people to make sure that the day's sermons had been both listened to and understood; they conducted the Friday Question meetings in the week of Communion, and, most important of all in regard to our present interest, no one was allowed to partake of the bread and wine without their express approval.

Yet, throughout the rural areas of Scotland, crowds flocked to any Communion festival that was within reach, and for five or more hours sat in the open air listening to a solid non-stop diet of preaching. It is only natural that we should wonder why; communion Sunday today still provokes a larger than normal attendance, but there is no parish-wide interest in the event, while those who attend partake fully and are not satisfied with the spectator's role. Our forefathers' devotion to the Sacrament was partly the result of personal fear and superstition and partly a consequence of the firm hold the minister could have over his flock. Apart from what the Church might provide, there was little happening in any parish on a Sunday and it would be wrong to discount a real sense of piety on the part of many worshippers; but a large part of the explanation for the great difference between the communion season now and 150 years ago lies in realising fully that the Communion was not merely a one-day event. Nor was it merely a religious festival.

Things began to warm up on the Thursday prior to the big Sunday with the holding of at least two services. Friday saw the Day of Questions, with a further two diets of public worship occupying much of Saturday. We have already seen something of the marathon that was Sunday, and the whole affair was rounded off with a final two services on the Monday. Attendances at the Thursday services were rarely large; even the preaching 'giants', in full training for the sacramental occasion, could hardly make two services occupy a full day. Increasingly, therefore, there came to be a holiday, almost a carnival-like, atmosphere about the place for much of the week-end. We quote Story again: 'The religious exercises were varied by a good deal of eating and drinking, whether in the open-air or in the nearest public-houses. An old clergyman of a parish near Rosneath used to remark with pride when an extra gathering attended his communion, "It was a creditable crood; there was fourteen stane o' saumon eaten in the village." '

One might disapprove of the unlikely combination of events that were accepted under the umbrella of this High and Holy Feast; one could scarcely pretend sorrow that the century saw many changes in this sphere; but with life in Scotland often grim and drab in the early years of last century, it is not surprising that this mixture of religion and revelry was very popular; nor should the Church's unparalleled opportunity of reaching vast crowds of ordinary people with the message of Christ be underestimated. In fairness, it should be recognised that the clergy themselves were not above indulging in worldly pleasures if opportunity were given. In particular, the officiating clergy traditionally enjoyed a grand dinner on the Monday to mark the end of the week's heroics, and on occasion this dinner might not appear to have been the most seemly end to a religious festival of such solemnity. One in Argyllshire in the second decade of the nineteenth century carries this report: 'We drank, roared and sang, fired our grapeshot (nothing less than royal port), and bumpered every young lady in the country. About eight in the evening, some were sick and others were groaning.'

The nineteenth century brought changes in the Sacramental pattern in two main directions. First, the season was curtailed to exclude the Thursday and Monday services, and, second, there was a growing feeling that the Sacrament should be celebrated not once only in each year on a grand scale, but several times each year with less attention to sheer size and length. This latter alteration was naturally more easily implemented in the towns than in the country areas where the parishioners had further to travel to get to Church, and where in any case radical change in something so sacred was more stubbornly resisted. So, for instance, as early as 1829, John Brown celebrated Communion every two months in Broughton Place Church, Edinburgh, and publicly advocated a weekly Sacrament. Nevertheless, things were moving in the country parishes also and the elder Story, before his death in 1859, had succeeded in introducing, first a second Communion Service in the year, and then a third. Before his son left the parish in 1886, the total was further boosted to four per year. Slowest to change were the true Highland areas; indeed even today the process is not complete in that there are still those there who feel that the Table is only for the godly few. Despite this, however, no less a figure than Donald John Martin of Stornoway took this stand in the 1880s: 'I would rather have one hundred at the Table who should not have been there than that one soul should be debarred whom Christ invited.'

There was throughout Scotland an increasingly pronounced wind of change blowing through the customs associated with the celebration of Holy Communion. Broadly speaking, there were three main reasons for the changes coming when they did. First, the scathing indictment of the abuses of the Sacramental occasion in Robert Burns' poem, 'The Holy Fair', was widely discussed and encouraged a frank analysis by people and ministers alike of practices hitherto accepted as hallowed. Secondly, the people of Scotland began to tire of five days' protracted preaching: other amusements offered more by way of entertainment, excitement and education. Thirdly, an increasing number of ministers realised that a different approach was needed to suit the changing attitudes and abilities of their parishioners: to this extent, the Church was a step ahead of popular opinion, actively initiating change rather than consenting to it because of public pressure and declining interest. It is worth noting that, as the Thursday and Monday services came to be forsaken as more people regarded these days as mere holidays, so the ministerial banquet gave way to a more seemly Sunday lunch in the manse.

Following the theme that, throughout the nineteenth century, parish ministers in the industrial areas of Scotland faced sizeable difficulties unknown to their country colleagues, one very basic difference in regard to the pastor–people relationship was recognised as early as 1797. In that year, Dr. Stevenson MacGill was inducted to Glasgow's Tron Church from the parish of Eastwood on the outskirts of the city. Writing of this change of sphere, his biographer, Robert Burns of Paisley, says, 'In a country charge, the people of the parish and the members of the congregation are generally speaking one, and the labours of the clergyman through the week are thus concentrated on those families whom he addresses from the pulpit on the Sabbath. It is different in a large town, where, from obvious circumstances, it is impossible to identify the two; and hence it is that the minister of a city parish becomes, almost by necessity, a pluralist; he has a large parish over whose ecclesiastical interests he must preside and whose families he must catechise and visit; in addition, he has a congregation which may or may not be gathered from the parochial locality and yet whose families he must make himself acquainted with by personal visitation if he desires to be really a useful minister to them.' This 'double-task', frequently too large for one man, even with an assistant, posed a constant problem, as indeed it still does today in our city-centre charges, and the over-burdened minister regularly had to choose between neglecting his members and ignoring his parishioners. Commenting in 1870 on the large number of Glaswegians who never attended Church, Professor Charteris clearly felt that all too often the parishioners were the losers: 'What are the ministers doing? They are incessantly engaged all the hours of the day and many of the night in keeping their congregations together, for it is considered that those who attend his church are a minister's stock-in-trade and that he must "mind his business".'

Such behaviour becomes more understandable in the light of a second main difference between town and country. In the early part of the nineteenth century, Scotland's towns did not possess sufficient Church buildings, or sufficient seats to house the rapidly expanding population. The country areas on the other hand were, generally speaking, adequately provided for: some of their churches were sub-standard as buildings – the historian Cunningham speaks of some with roofs in daily danger of collapse, and of too many still with earthen floors and no seating. A few parishes in the western highlands had had no church since the Reformation. Nevertheless, the country areas could, by and large, boast church accommodation adequate for the population's needs, even if the whole population were regularly to attend worship. The towns, however, were very different. When Chalmers went to Glasgow Tron in 1816, the population of Glasgow was three times what it had been thirty years earlier, yet no new church had been built. So far as Edinburgh was concerned, the Government Commission of 1838 reported that there was room then for only forty-eight per cent of the population within the existing churches. The ministers, then, feeling a natural responsibility to those who attended their Churches, and finding the duties involved in this more than sufficient to occupy their time, cannot too hastily be condemned for failing to launch massive parish missions especially if their buildings were already comfortably filled.

What was needed was a planned scheme of new building so that town parishes could be reduced to manageable proportions and ministers be able to establish active contact with both parish and congregation. With this present study being concerned with the individual parish minister's response to the problems facing him and not with national Church policy, we note simply two factors in the Church Extension programme – the drive of Chalmers and his Church Extension Committee, and the formation of the Free Church. Between 1835 and 1841, Chalmers's committee saw 222 new churches opened, while in the first two years of the Free Church's existence, no less than 500 new buildings were dedicated.

One point that emerges, however, is very relevant. With too few men and too few churches, we might expect that there would have been those in the towns whom the minister could not reach and who would remain outwith the Church. It is, however, disturbing that those who were thus outwith the Church belonged almost exclusively to one class, namely the poor. Three examples from the 1830s illustrate this very clearly. In this period, Robert McCheyne carried out a survey in two poorer areas of Edinburgh, the Lawnmarket and the Canongate, and discovered that less than one in seven of the inhabitants had any active Church connection. Thomas Guthrie, coming to the similarly poor parish of Old Greyfriars as colleague to Mr. Sym in 1837, found that in the first 150 homes he visited, there were not as many as five people in regular attendance at any house of God. In Glasgow, in a survey carried out during the building of Cambridge Street U.P. Church, it was shown that only five per cent of the inhabitants of the Port Dundas area of the city went to any Church.

A similar situation is exemplified in the ministry of Thomas Chalmers in the new St. John's Church in Glasgow. Moving to this charge from the Tron in 1819, Chalmers regularly preached to crowded congregations: St. John's quickly became one of the wealthiest and most prosperous churches in the country; and yet, within its parish area, more than one in three of the adult population had not even a nominal connection with any Church, while in the parishioners' homes stark poverty was an everyday reality. St. John's congregations were almost entirely composed of the wealthier classes who travelled considerable distances to hear the fine preaching on offer: to reach those round the Church doors needed a special conscious drive by Chalmers and his elders.

There is no single reason for this gulf between the poorer classes and the Church. Norman Macleod said that in the years before his induction to Loudoun, the Church there was regarded as 'Tory, aristocracy, and middle-class farmer', with the result that the poorer folk, whose heroes were Tom Paine and Robert Burns, gave it a consistently wide berth. In the same way, those who were condemned in the towns to live in overcrowded conditions on near poverty incomes generally saw the Church as the preserve of the middle and upper classes and kept well clear. On a different level, while Church offerings were not a regular burden on the worshipper early in the nineteenth century, there were other items of expenditure which the less-well-off could ill afford. As Thomas Guthrie remarked, 'You cannot ask one to go to the City Chamberlain and pay 6/– for a seat who would bless you for six pennies to buy meal for his children.' Seat rents were high, and this, together with the expensive mode of dress deemed necessary for attendance at Church, meant that many who might have wished to go to worship felt debarred.

At the same time, the ministers themselves were not without blame in many instances for the absence from the pews of the poor. Overwork and congregational responsibilities do not tell the whole story, for too many of them shrank from the distasteful business of visiting the wretched homes in which these people had to live; too few were willing to risk losing their wealthier 'gathered' congregation by drawing in those who were so unequal socially. James Begg, minister of Newington Free Church, was one who did undertake vigorous work in this direction. One of his visits is vividly described in a letter published in 1849: 'We plunged into a black opening more like the mouth of a coalpit than the entrance to human habitations; we were almost knocked down by the horrid vapour by which we were assailed; the population of the ruinous tenement was greater than that of a considerable country village, and these human beings were in far more uncomfortable and wretched circumstances than any sensible farmer's cattle.' If anything, conditions in Glasgow were worse, so that ministerial behaviour of the sort described by Thomas Guthrie can be understood if not condoned: 'Once a year he approached the mouth of each several "close" in his district – down whose dark vista of sin and misery, however, he never penetrated – and there, uncovering his head with due solemnity, and lifting his gloved right hand, he besought the Divine blessing to rest on "all the inhabitants, young and old, of this close". The annual "visitation" thus ended, he went on his way.'

If additional accommodation and man-power were needed, so also was some means whereby the poorer parishioners could attend worship without expense or embarrassment. There was, too, a clear need for the Church, nationally and through its parish ministers, to work actively for the dramatic improvement of the conditions under which the poor had to live. Thomas Chalmers was perhaps the first to make the Church more easily available to the poor in that he introduced in St. John's a third Sunday service, in the evening, which was to be attended only by the poor. Thomas Guthrie followed suit as colleague in Old Greyfriars, holding Sunday afternoon services in the Magdalene Chapel in the Cowgate where the poor parishioners were admitted first and free of charge, and where passers-by enjoyed the rare spectacle of the better-off queuing to take any places that remained. Moving to the new St. John's Church in Edinburgh in 1840, Guthrie extended this idea, reserving all 650 seats in the area for parishioners; such was the success of this arrangement that demand quickly outstripped supply so that week by week many got in where they could, and many worshippers clambered on to the roof and sat round the ventilating apertures. Such people could not hope to see the service as it progressed: their 'pews' were rough planks laid across the rafters: the air they had to breathe was foul; yet without fail they came, eager to hear the preacher who so obviously cared for them.

Outstanding, however, in this move to take the Church to the poor and bring the poor to the Church was Norman Macleod. In Loudoun, where, as we saw, his mid-week lectures enjoyed genuine popular success, he began an evening service for those who 'excused themselves from going to Church at the ordinary hour on account of having no suitable clothing'. Moving to Dalkeith in 1843, he tackled a similar problem by establishing a fund to provide clothes for the thirty or so parishioners who genuinely lacked Church attire, but it was not until he moved to Glasgow's Barony Church in 1851 that he was able to involve the poor of the parish in the life of the Church to something like the extent he wished. In 1857, for example, he introduced evening services where none were admitted who were not in working clothes; he even stationed a 'posse of elders' at the door to turn away anyone showing too great signs of respectability. An English newspaper reporter, anxious to cover this aspect of Macleod's work, went to great lengths to assume working-class disguise, and even then he was worried that the scrutineers might detect that his hair was suspiciously tidy. In principle Macleod was never in favour of segregating worshippers according to wealth and social position, but as a short-term expedient to counter a difficult situation, he saw its merits. Certainly the folk of the Barony parish approved: 'The pews were filled with men in fustian jackets and women, bareheaded, or with an old shawl drawn over their head, and dressed, most of them, in short gown and petticoat.' Elsewhere in Glasgow and Edinburgh, ministers began to realise that their churches could be both preaching stations to which would travel the wealthy, and true parish churches for all irrespective of rank. It is little wonder that Macleod entered this enthusiastic note in his journal: 'By God's mercy I have crammed the church with people in working clothes. This is grand. I do not envy Wellington at Waterloo.' Incidentally, it is surely worth noting in passing that enthusiasm for these services was not confined to ecclesiastical circles. The Glasgow police, for instance, reported that not infrequently well-known thieves were present to hear Macleod, and they willingly attested that many hundreds of lives were, through his services, 'reclaimed from lawless habits', a fact that is in some measure supported by a comment from the aforementioned English journalist who expressed surprise that the pew cushions were left in place and the Bibles and Psalm Books not removed prior to the evening services. It is, he said, 'a plain proof that, by the test of several years, the poor could be trusted'.

This belated, if sincere, interest in their spiritual welfare, however, could only go so far in convincing the poor that the Church really did care for them: clearly, the Church had to bestir itself in two other directions also. It had to show active concern for the improvement of their housing, and it had to provide activities for their leisure time. Now, in such a large matter as housing, we might expect that progress would have most readily been achieved through pressure from the Church as a whole so that it would properly be a topic outwith our present concern; but this is not entirely so. Admittedly, the Church of Scotland's Commission on the Religious Condition of the People, which reported in 1896, dealt with poverty and housing: Glasgow Presbytery appointed a Commission on the Housing of the Poor which 'did good work in at least calling attention to a crying necessity': but individual ministers, on their own initiative, showed the way time after time. Men like James Begg and W. G. Blaikie did what they could to tackle the problem nationwide: Begg took a leading part in the formation of the Edinburgh Co-operative Building Society in 1861; he persuaded the Government to include a question in the census of that year asking the number of apartments in each house; and he never ceased to publicise facts and figures showing appalling overcrowding with as many as seven and eight adults regularly living in one single room. Blaikie, for his part, published a book, 'Better conditions for the working classes', which sold in vast numbers and became a standard work on the subject. On the other hand, ministers like William Mackenzie of North Leith

Free Church tackled the housing problems of their own parishes and accomplished a great deal despite obviously limited financial resources. Mackenzie was the first to involve a congregation in the actual business of erecting houses 'of a superior kind' for the poor, and as many as ten were completed. In the neighbouring parish of Pilrig Free, Blaikie seized on the same idea, building four rows of cottages in Leith Walk by 1862: in this project, sixty-two homes were erected at a cost of £7,000, the average annual rental of each being £7.

Understandably, however, this kind of work could not be tackled by many kirk sessions, and the more general move at parish level was to provide attractive accommodation and worthwhile activities for the poorer parishioners' enjoyment outwith working hours. With conditions in many homes made intolerable through squalor and overcrowding, no one spent any longer in them than was absolutely necessary. In the early years of the nineteenth century, however, the only refuge was the public house. Concerts were few and far between: during the two winters which Alexander Carlyle spent as a student in Glasgow (1743–1745), that town had only one concert – it was given by a violinist assisted by two dancing-school fiddlers and the town-waits – and even as late as 1870, Edinburgh had only two concerts in a full year. In any case, additional concerts would scarcely have provided the poorer classes with entertainment to their taste. Similarly, the few lectures which there were in the large towns did not appeal. The result was that the numerous public houses enjoyed a virtual monopoly of the working classes' free time.

With the Church, however, becoming more alive to its responsibilities to this section of society, this situation could not be allowed to continue. There were problems, nevertheless, which were daunting. Suitable Church Hall accommodation was almost entirely lacking; there was no established net-work of week-night activities which could be adapted to appeal to those whose second home was by tradition the public house; alcohol had a vice-like grip on the working classes of the towns which could not easily be broken. In this last regard, statistics quoted by Dr. Stewart Mechie give a measure of the challenge: in Glasgow and Edinburgh in the 1830s, there was on average one licence to every 14 or 15 homes, with one quarter of the working classes' earnings going to the licensees; referring to 1840, we are told that '30,000 people in Glasgow are drunk every Saturday night', and not just drunk, but 'in a brutal state of intoxication'. Thomas Guthrie, visiting the parishioners of Old Greyfriars, Edinburgh, in the 1830s reckoned that nine-tenths of the poverty, wretchedness, and Sabbath breaking that he found was traceable to 'that detestable vice of drunkenness'.

Little wonder that Guthrie was one of the pioneers in seeking to provide, through the local churches, adequate alternative attractions which might weaken the hold of the public house. To this end, he patronised, in 1855, a series of cheap concerts on Saturday evenings in which singers, pianists, and violinists provided entertainment for those who would never have gone near an orchestral concert. Going further, he opened working men's clubs which were in effect public houses without drink, offering comradeship, warmth and spaciousness which the private house could not give, but without the drunken aftermath. Norman Macleod worked to the same formula in Glasgow when he established a most successful refreshment room – the first of several in the city – where, in alcohol-free surroundings, working men could get food, well-cooked, at cheap prices, and where there was a comfortable reading-room. Similarly popular was the 'Holly Tree', opened by Charteris in the Tolbooth Church, Edinburgh, where, with tea, coffee, a reading room and a games room, the inhabitants of the Lawnmarket found more than a home from home, and where as many as 400 customers could be counted in a single day. In the 1880s, Donald John Martin imported this idea to Stornoway with, in his case, the added 'bonus' that his coffee shops were opened in what had been the area's two pubs, Martin having bought the property at his own expense. At a later point, we shall take note of the Temperance Movement; in some areas pressure from local clergy brought about the complete closure of public houses; for the moment, however, it is clear that without recourse to prohibition, without even a self-imposed policy of total abstinence, ministers, and their kirk sessions, were showing not only a willingness but a determination to compete with the public house for those whom they had almost entirely neglected just a few years before.

Turning to the lack of week-night activities centred on the

parish church, the emergence of certain week-night classes held within Church premises in which the poor and uneducated parishioners were offered training in the basic disciplines and skills necessary to raise their standards of life is also relevant. Prominent in organising these classes were James Begg, two of the Robertson brothers, and Norman Macleod. Begg, minister of the Middle Church, Paisley, from 1831 to 1835, detailed one of his missionary assistants to conduct evening classes in English, reading, writing and arithmetic. William Robertson, minister of Irvine U.P. Church from 1843 to 1886, and his elder brother James, minister of Newington, Edinburgh, organised teams of office-bearers and members from their congregations to carry out similar work, while Norman Macleod, with classes of over 200 enrolled, had a staff of fully certificated teachers. In these classes, 'the interesting spectacle was presented of grown-up men and women, many of them married, patiently toiling at different standards from the alphabet upwards'.

At the same time as these 'crash courses' were being successfully introduced for the adult population of the town's poorer quarters, individual churches and their ministers were beginning to provide systematic education for the children of these areas who might otherwise have grown up no better equipped to succeed in life than were their parents. It had been the great aim of the Reformers that each parish should have its school and that all children should attend; in the towns in the early nineteenth century, however, this aim was far from being realised. The influx of families from the country areas posed numerical problems, and the parents' indifference to education and reluctance to pay school fees meant that the whole system was breaking down. In 1872, the State took from the Church complete responsibility for education in Scotland, with the result that the whole matter is lifted outwith our present study, but before that date certain individual ministers had begun to tackle this problem at their own local levels, often with remarkable results.

The pioneer in this field was Dr. Andrew Thomson who was inducted to St. George's, Edinburgh, in 1814. He had a school built in connection with that Church; he himself taught for a time in its classes; and he compiled several of its text books. On a larger scale, Thomas Chalmers, while in St. John's, Glasgow, provided schools for 700 of the poorer children of his parish, charging fees much lower than normal. Not surprisingly, Norman Macleod was well to the fore in this work, so that, in a period of ten years, he was able to provide 2000 additional school places for the underprivileged. He also devised a scheme whereby children from the Barnhill Poorhouse were boarded out with decent-living, respectable folk so that their education would not only be in the academic sphere. Most successful, however, in his efforts to educate the poor was Thomas Guthrie. In many ways his work was more national than parochial – it most certainly had nation-wide repercussions – and yet his schools were established originally on a parish basis. In 1845 he published a circular drawing attention to the fact that in the three previous years, 740 children under 14 (245 under 10) had been committed to prison. He further estimated that in Edinburgh at that time 1000 boys and girls were growing up 'ignorant in the midst of knowledge, savages in the midst of civilisation, heathens in the midst of Christianity'. By 1847, he had established three of his 'Ragged Schools' where, free of charge, 265 children received 'porridge and broth as well as a sound education'. These schools, hailed by the author Thackeray as 'the finest sight in Edinburgh', gave an all-round education, provided clothes where needed, fed nourishing meals, and even afforded the rudiments of industrial training.

What these schools achieved no one can ever fully estimate: they were certainly the making of many children who otherwise would never have risen above the squalor of their infant surroundings, and they demonstrated clearly to the Church and to the country what could and should be done. One set of figures is well worth noting: in 1847, the year in which the Ragged Schools were founded, 'over five per cent of the prisoners in Edinburgh were under 14, while in 1851, the number had fallen to less than one per cent'. This surely was not coincidence alone, but further proof of what Guthrie and his colleagues were doing.

If Guthrie's schemes were the most successful in assisting the poorer children, the most novel idea came from the home of W. G. Blaikie, the ministerial house-builder of Pilrig. We could fairly omit all reference to this as it was master-minded by his wife in that period when he was a Professor in New College and therefore outwith the parish ministry; nevertheless, it shows what one determined individual, in the name of the Church, could accomplish. Mrs. Blaikie's twin aims were to help the rising generations to a better life and at the same time alleviate the problems of overcrowding in the towns. She therefore launched a scheme in the 1860s whereby children were taken from homes in the towns, where the parents' poverty or drunkenness made their lives intolerable, and were settled with decent families in Canada. This may seem callous even although children were not 'exported' without parental permission, but the scheme was popular and, by all accounts, of lasting benefit to the children: the greatest number of children leaving the country in this way in any one year was 809.

So, as the nineteenth century ended, the yawning gap between the Church and the poor of Scotland's towns was closing. Comparison with the rural parish in this regard would always be unfavourable. Not even a Norman Macleod could hope to establish the person-to-person contact with his numerous and constantly changing parishioners that his country colleagues took for granted; much as Thomas Chalmers did, as we shall see, to assist materially the poor living near St. John's, he could not begin to provide for them in the distinctive and personal way that was open to his rural brethren. Andrew Thomson in Sprouston, Roxburghshire, for example, had his glebe sown with oats to be sold at cost price to his parishioners in a time of scarcity. Henry Duncan in Ruthwell, Dumfriesshire, had a corn boat sent from Liverpool and sold its contents at cost price; he countered local unemployment by giving work on his glebe to those who were idle; and he brought cartloads of flax from Dumfries for the womenfolk to spin when times were hard. But the fact remains that, with more and more town ministers prepared to work hard for the all-round welfare of their poorer parishioners, a mighty link had been forged which could not easily be broken; the Church had begun truly to gain the ear and the confidence of a whole new congregation.

It is not, however, the case that, while the poor were universally absent from the town churches until positive steps were taken to draw them in, the wealthier classes not only flocked to the Church but more than adequately filled all the available accommodation. Things were never as clear-cut. The biographer of Andrew Thomson, for instance, states that in the years before Thomson came to Edinburgh in 1810, 'it had been the fashion of the gentlemen of the city to despise going to Church – they left Church-going to the ladies'. It was not the poorer males of the city who are here described. Further, there was no general conviction among the well-to-do who did attend Church that their local parish church was the one to be supported; rather they travelled to whatever pulpits currently took their fancy. So the Guthries and the Macleods had churches bursting at the seams while others, lacking popularity with the itinerant rich and no more successful than their competitors in capturing the poor round their doors, had a distinctly abandoned look. For much of the nineteenth century, the town churches did present these two sharply contrasting pictures: the Government Commission of 1838 reported that there were 11,000 unlet sittings in the Church of Scotland buildings in Edinburgh and a further 9000 sittings unlet on the Dissenters' side – all this, as we saw, at a time when there was only Church accommodation in the capital for forty-eight per cent of the population; Glasgow was no better, and Cameron Lees of St. Giles' Cathedral speaks of Churches in that city where, so poor was the attendance at worship, that 'you might fire a gun and hit no one'.

On the other hand, there were the great preaching-stations which, although the congregations were 'gathered' in terms of wealth and came from all over the surrounding area, demonstrated our ancestors' interest in what the Church was doing and saying. For instance, Rose Street Secession Church in Edinburgh was the scene of many a remarkable crowd during the seven-year ministry of John Brown in the 1820s. On Sundays, this preacher had frequently to be led from the session house to the pulpit across the tops of the pews, so many were the worshippers crowding the passages and stairs. Public enthusiasm for his week-night lectures was on a similar scale, even although his lecture themes – one notable crowd-puller being on 'Uriah the Hittite' – were not such as we today would readily term 'popular'; and his beadle, James Chalmers, had to be proof against the half-crowns offered by ladies anxious to get in before the doors opened. Incidentally, it seems that all Brown's beadles were the better of qualifications in crowd control, because when he moved to Broughton Place, the combination of vast crowds and poor ventilation within the Church left the harassed official with an unusually large number of fainting cases. Here at least, however, his work was not without its lighter side by virtue of the remedy prescribed to revive the casualties – 'He cut their stay laces which ran before the knife and cracked like a bow-string.' (If fainting cases were a source of disturbance to those inside the Church, there were occasions when they were a blessing to those still outside.) J. P. Struthers of Greenock tells of his own attempts to hear Dr. Alexander Whyte on one of his tours; when he arrived at the Church, all the seats were taken and the doors were shut. Struthers was informed by a spectator that the building was crammed and that hundreds, unable to gain entry, had gone home. 'Well', said Struthers, 'if the building is so full as that, somebody will be sure to turn faint, and then will be my chance.' Accordingly, he kept running round the Church, watching the various doors, until indeed one person was conveyed out of the building by two of her friends. He took his chance, went in, and 'heard such words from Dr. Whyte as I trust I shall never forget'.

Similar tales could be told of churches in all the main towns and cities whenever a great orator held the pulpit. In 1836, for example, Robert Murray McCheyne instituted Dundee's first mid-week prayer meeting in St. Peter's Church, and the novelty, coupled with the personality of this spiritual giant, drew regular attendances of over 800. Principal Caird was inducted to Lady Yester's, Edinburgh, in 1847, and to the West Park Chapel, Glasgow, ten years later. In both Churches, he preached to congregations that more than filled every pew. In Edinburgh, a large number of the morning congregation actually remained in their places after the benediction to be sure of their seat for the afternoon, while in Glasgow, 'each week crowds queued outside and were grateful to obtain standing room'. Up in Aberdeen, Greyfriars Church welcomed vast crowds throughout the ministry of David McTaggart (1848–1857): on several occasions police were needed to keep control of the crowds waiting for the doors to open, while at the annual letting of seats, the presence of the constabulary was an absolute necessity. Seat rents were, as we remarked, much too high in relation to the working man's wages, but in such churches, it often took several years before a whole family succeeded in gaining seats, such was the demand.

So, within the towns, both rich and poor had to be drawn to Church: no parish minister could here depend simply on his rank or authority to fill the pews. Where, however, the ministers did make the effort to attract the poor, where the orator did faithfully exercise his talents, then the people of Scotland were not indifferent; whether in town or country, our forefathers could be brought to a generous response to the voice of Christ through His Church.

Chapter 3

There is one Lord, one faith, one baptism

In Scotland in the nineteenth century, several major ecclesiastical 'incidents', though national in consequence, inevitably coloured the Church's person to person contact at parish level.

Supreme in this category was the Great Disruption which, in 1843, split the Church in Scotland into the Old Established Church and the new Free Church. We have already seen how intense could be the hatred between the rival factions, the Moderates and the Evangelicals. It is now time to examine the extent to which the bond between the individual minister and his congregation was strong enough to withstand the splitting of the National Church. The issue was whether the minister normally had such a hold over his people that, even in such a vital matter, his decision would, almost automatically, be their decision; or whether the congregation's clearly expressed choice influenced the minister in making up his own mind.

One thing is certain: the men and women in the pews were genuinely interested in the disputes which led eventually to the Disruption. This can hardly be surprising when the principal debate centred on the workings of Patronage, which gave the Patron of a parish the right to force a minister on the congregation even where the whole congregation had expressed themselves opposed to the presentee. In 1841, for instance, John Edwards was inducted to the parish of Marnoch when only one member of the congregation, the local tavern-keeper, had signed his call. With several inductions equally bitterly contested in the years before the Disruption, those who took their Church membership seriously could not be indifferent to any struggle whose outcome would directly affect their own democratic rights and privileges. Furthermore, the choice facing each minister was bound to affect each worshipper whether he liked it or not. In any large split within the National Church, many congregations would either find themselves without ministers, or else, if they chose to 'go out' with their pastors, they would be faced with finding from their own pockets the money to pay stipends and erect churches, manses and schools. They had, too, a real personal worry: the majority of the lairds sat with the Moderates, so that many a working man could stand to lose both house and job if he threw in his lot with the Evangelicals.

If there was any remaining doubt as to whether the average occupant of the pew would take a deep interest in the pre-Disruption skirmishes, the manner in which the debates were carried on settled the issue. Sunday by Sunday, the parish pulpits became platforms from which, in bold and often provocative language, the evils of the opposing party were denounced. Day by day, the leading personalities on both sides were touring the country drumming up vast crowds to hear and discuss the principles at stake. Henry Duncan, for example, spoke to 1000 in Huntly in 1840, a number which did not wholly satisfy the enthusiastic sponsors of the gathering: 'I was told', said Duncan, 'that the coldness and threatening aspect of the weather had kept numbers away.' A similar crowd stood for two and a half hours in a barn in Stenton near Haddington to hear Dr. Guthrie. 2000 attended a debate in the Abbey Church, Arbroath, and showed their enthusiasm for the Evangelical cause by drowning out all opposing speakers with their hissing and drumming of sticks. In the West Church, Edinburgh, at a time when the Disruption seemed inevitable, no less than 3200 turned out to hear Dr. Candlish. Quite clearly the ordinary worshippers were concerned; they felt involved, and they sought to be informed.

An analysis of the actual results of the Disruption shows, however, that in the majority of cases the congregations, almost to a man, took the same line as did their ministers, so that what happened, for example, in Loudoun was repeated in many parishes throughout the land. There, Norman Macleod addressed his congregation for three and a half hours on why they should not join the Free Church; in all that time, 'not a soul moved' and almost everyone chose to remain with their pastor in the Established Church. In the Highlands, particularly, minister and people acted as one. In these areas, individual ministries could be of very long duration. A minister could frequently be succeeded by his son, thus ensuring continuity of ideas and affections, and therefore in a very real way much of the loyalty formerly shown to clan chiefs had transferred itself to the ministers who were, in their areas, virtual kings and bishops. As late as 1875, Dr. James MacGregor of St. Cuthbert's, Edinburgh, made this comment on Church life in the north of Scotland: 'The people were in the grip of a zealous but intensely bitter order of Free Church ministers, and they followed their bidding with a loyalty as blindly devoted as ever they had given to their feudal chieftains.' So, for example, in Sutherland, where the clergy were virtually one hundred per cent behind the Disruption, out of a population of 25,000 only 219 remained within the Established Church. The people of Lewis reacted in a similar way with only 460 out of 23,000 declining to 'go out' with their ministers.

In the towns, the situation was inevitably rather different. The gathered congregations, for example, had, in the years prior to the final split in 1843, allied themselves to ministers whose views they accepted and therefore massive upheavals here were unnecessary; elsewhere, with often a variety of churches to choose from at no great distance from one's home, transfers of affection were reasonably easily effected. But whether in town or country, one thing is undeniable: the tie between minister and people was very considerably strengthened as a result of the events of 1843. On the one hand, the ministers who joined the Free Church felt a real debt of gratitude to their people who sacrificed so much to maintain them and provide churches; on the other hand, the congregations gained a new respect for men who were willing to turn their back on security for themselves and their families for a cause in which they believed. Even the Established Church, though it took some years to recover from the loss of close on 500 of its ordained ministers, rose to new strength made all the greater by the firmer bond that existed between pastor and flock determined to maintain the Auld Kirk.

Regrettably, however, at the same time as individual ministers and their congregations were coming closer together, the two conflicting groups of clergymen were moving further apart, and the hostility was rapidly spreading to their congregations. The more inflamed ministers of the Free Church felt called to denounce the Established Kirk as 'a stinking pond', 'a common sewer', ' a house full of rats'. Hugh Miller, the influential editor of the Free Church Journal, *The Witness*, offered this advice, 'Let the parish minister be regarded as virtually the one excommunicated man in the district, the man with whom no one is to join in prayer, whose Church is to be avoided as an impure and unholy place, whose addresses are not to be listened to, who is everywhere to be put under the ban of the community.' It is unquestionably sad to think of this being construed by any as 'Christian' advice; it is infinitely sadder to see that the two sets of ministers responded readily in many parishes and 'passed each other on the road as if plague-stricken'. Not unnaturally, their enthusiastic supporters needed no second invitation to emphasise their own solidarity and their support for their ministers, so that, almost as a holy duty, the most devout would plot and scheme mischief for the opposition. Going to an induction in Uig shortly after the Disruption, the ministers representing Lewis Presbytery of the Church of Scotland could find no one willing to row their boat; even to do this for clergy of the Established Church would have been a mortal sin. The ministers, therefore, had to row themselves, almost drowning half-way because a staunch Free-Kirker had seen it as his solemn duty to remove the plug from their boat. Even the traditional peace of the Lord's Day was frequently shattered as rival groups passed each other on the road to their respective churches.

At times, words were scarcely adequate artillery as is seen from this snatch of conversation recorded by the elder Story one Sabbath in Rosneath; 'Was it no' a mercy it was the Sabbath Day and a borrow't umbrella that I had in my haun', or as sure's death, I would ha' felled him.' The Scots are traditionally tight with their money; domestic servants in the 1840s were none too generously paid; but, as W. G. Blaikie shows us, it was considered wiser to be poor than to touch 'tainted' silver. Betty Ross, as impecunious as many manse maids, was left money in her cousin's will, but not even the threat of the poor house would have let her draw a penny piece of it, because the deceased had been a minister of the loathsome Moderate Party. In many parts of Scotland, feelings ran so high that 'the very boys at school ranged themselves into hostile camps of

Moderates and Non-Intrusionists' and many a bloody battle was fought in mini-assemblies convened in the playground. In 1864, Norman Macleod, visiting Ross and Sutherland, summed up the situation as follows: 'The feelings of the Free Church to the Establishment are hardly equalled by those of the Roman Catholics in Galway to a Protestant missionary, or those of the Mohammedans in Damascus to a Christian.' Eleven years later, Dr. MacGregor of St. Cuthbert's could find no improvement: 'If the Apostle Paul had preached from the pulpits of the National Church, no Highlander belonging to the Free Church would have believed himself orthodox had he crossed the threshold to hear him.' As late as 1886, a Free Church missionary wrote to his friend, 'My first object is to win souls to Christ, my second is to smash the Church.'

Perhaps the saddest aftermath of the Disruption, so far as the minister-people relationship was concerned, was the fact that in countless small towns and villages, where hitherto the Church had been a focal point of parish unity, and where the minister had successfully been the great friend in common to young and old, rich and poor, the events of 1843 split the community in two. The new Free Churches, which were so speedily erected, brought bitter rivalries and, in the name of Christ, age-old friendships and associations were shattered. Where before the minister had been able to equate his congregation with his parish, there was now a competitive intolerant congregationalism. Elsewhere, as for example in the Highlands, where the swing to the Free Church was well nigh total, the incoming ministers of the Established Church had the heartbreaking task of trying to exercise a Christian ministry in a hostile community where the basic courtesies were denied him by rival pastor and flock alike. It is not uncommon to read of Old Kirk congregations never out of single figures in the years following the Disruption; many a kirk session could not meet at all because perhaps only one elder remained loyal to the old dispensation; frequently, buildings fell into a sorry state of disrepair. The first post-Disruption offering in Holburn Church, Aberdeen, totalled three halfpennies.

John Cairns may have been right when he affirmed that the Disruption was 'one of the greatest blessings to the Church of Christ and to the world'. It can be argued that the debates, bitter though they often were, turned the ordinary man's mind to thoughts of religion. Certainly the ties between minister and congregation were in many ways strengthened by the ongoing events. But the sad thought remains that though the two denominations' ministers and people might fiercely protest that they did what they did in love of Christ, they had not really begun in any numbers to love their fellow men. There was more than a little truth in the joking aside of Cameron Lees who, describing a visit he paid to Egypt and the Holy Land, says, 'On reaching Calais, I asked a fellow-traveller, a priest, whether he knew of Dr. Begg or Dr. Candlish, and on his shaking his head by way of negation, I felt I had at last got into a Christian country.'

The second ecclesiastical 'incident' of the nineteenth century might more correctly be described as a series of incidents. In this period, several notable heresy cases came before the Assemblies and generated a good deal of lay interest: in some instances, indeed, this interest was such that it directly affected a pastor's relationship with his people. John McLeod Campbell, inducted to the parish of Row (now called Rhu), Dunbartonshire, in 1825, was deposed by the General Assembly in 1831 for adhering to views on the Atonement which were judged to conflict with orthodoxy. The rights and wrongs of this judgment are not our concern: what is significant is the fact that a petition was presented to the Assembly signed by nineteen-twentieths of his parishioners expressing their 'affection and regard' for him as a minister and pastor. Furthermore, this strong bond was not destroyed by the ruling that heresy was held to be proved; rather McLeod Campbell's following, local and national, increased after he was deposed. No doubt notoriety played its part; the people would be curious to see and hear a heretic; but the personality and sincerity of the man ensured that he would be no seven days' wonder. So he preached in a tent in Bonhill in 1831 to a crowd of 2000; the same number gathered on an Oban moor; a Greenock Churchyard somehow accommodated 6000 to hear him. It is all the more remarkable that from 1833 until ill-health forced his retirement in 1859, he preached successfully to an independent congregation meeting in Glasgow's Lyceum Hall. An edict was issued to be read in all churches warning of the dangers of hearing him and even threatening withdrawal of the Sacraments from any who disobeyed; initially, this would only serve to heighten curiosity and so increase crowds, but his prolonged success, and the unswerving devotion of the people of Row, unquestionably show that in the hearts of many men and women in Scotland at this time, the man was more important than the message.

The cases of Robertson Smith and Edward Irving are rather different. Smith, a Free Church Professor in Aberdeen at the age of 23, was never a parish minister, and was deposed for views, mainly on the authorship of sections of the Old Testament, which were out of line with Free Church thinking. Irving, a former assistant to Chalmers in St. John's, was excommunicated by London Presbytery before being expelled by the Church of Scotland. It is sufficient to note again the vast public interest shown in both of these men. For example, on a flying visit to Edinburgh in 1828, Irving drew large crowds to a lecture on the Book of Revelation held at the unlikely hour of 5 a.m., while at his meeting in Kirkcaldy on the same trip, the crowds were such that the gallery of the Church collapsed, killing 35 people. All this merely underlines the fact that, more and more, the people of Scotland were able and anxious to think for themselves, regardless of what any official body might decree; it makes it increasingly obvious, also, that the time was gone when a combination of 'the minister's word and accepted practice' could expect to carry the day.

The other feature of the nineteenth century which had a direct bearing on the parish minister's involvement with his flock was the number of religious revivals that shook Scotland in this period. They came in three main waves. In 1839 and immediately after, there was the movement which began in Kilsyth and then spread to Dundee, Perth, Aberdeen and beyond. The leaders here were all ministers of the Established Church – W. C. Burns, Robert Murray McCheyne, John Milne, Alexander Somerville – and with the exception of Burns, all were parish ministers at the time. In 1858, parish ministers were once more involved – Moody Stuart, for example – but for the first time in Scotland, compelling lay evangelists were the main orators. The third surge of revival began in 1873 and revolved round the imported American genius of Moody and Sankey.

It is important to see how the parish minister in general

reacted to these awakenings, to gauge his measure of involvement, and to discover what lasting benefits were experienced by the Church at grass-roots. The scent of revival was not new in Kilsyth – the people there had joined in the Cambuslang awakening in 1742 when George Whitefield was prominent – and indeed it was at a service to commemorate this earlier revival that the first stirrings of the new movement were seen. W. C. Burns, whose father was the parish minister, preached a powerful sermon, intimating at its close a follow-up meeting on the Tuesday morning. For this, the Church was crowded to capacity and the enthusiasm was such that the meeting could not be concluded until five hours of worship and preaching had been completed. Alexander Smellie comments that the people were wonderfully stirred, the pubs were forsaken, and all saw that 'the age of Christ's miracles was not past'.

Returning to Dundee where he was deputising for Murray McCheyne in St. Peter's Church, Burns again lit the fire of revival so that crowded meetings were held each night for several weeks, with additional prayer meetings in private homes. Perth, too, was stirred under John Milne, minister of the town's St. Leonard's Church, and with Burns actively assisting, some incredible scenes were witnessed. It was not uncommon to see more people queued up outside the Church an hour before the start of the meetings than would have several times filled the Church, and on one occasion at least, the stampede for seats was so great when the doors were opened that several people were injured. One common factor in all these meetings was length. Beginning at 10 a.m. they could regularly go right through until 3 p.m., with a second 'house' lasting from 6 p.m. until the small hours of the following morning. Always these meetings were supplemented with home prayer groups which drew in both young and old to an unaccustomed show of overt piety. As Islay Burns, the brother of the Evangelist, says, 'The mountain glen, the solitary haugh, even the noisy loom shop became vocal often with the sounds of prayer and praise, or witnessed the solemn converse of brethren who at eventide talked with burning hearts of the things that had come to pass in those days.'

After Perth was well and truly alight, Burns moved north to Aberdeen where his preaching met with similar startling success. Some of the mill girls, for example, were seen to take their

Bibles to work as a result of his influence, and this was certainly something that had never been witnessed before. Glasgow was not so affected in this Revival movement as were the cities further north, but here too a few parish ministers went all out to present the Gospel challenge in the style favoured by Burns and Milne. In Anderston Parish, for example, the Rev. Alexander Somerville held meetings each weeknight except Saturday over a period of three months, and the public response was considerable.

The 1839 Revival was entirely home-grown, with parish ministers taking the initiative. In 1858, however, the leading speakers were travelling lay evangelists; at the same time, they did work in close co-operation with those parish ministers who were in sympathy with their aims and methods, and the Free Church, by this time firmly established, gave the whole an official approval which no denomination had been able to give the earlier movement. For example, Cunningham, Moderator of the Free Church in 1859, described it as 'the greatest movement since the Reformation'. The main centre of activities was St. Luke's Free Church in Edinburgh where the minister, Alexander Moody Stuart, gave wholehearted encouragement. Elsewhere it spread to Glasgow and Aberdeen and Perth where once again John Milne, inducted for a second time to St. Leonard's after a spell in Calcutta, took over the City Hall and for 70 nights filled it to capacity.

The third series of revivals centred on the visits to Scotland of Moody and Sankey in 1873, 1881, and 1891, and again the chief welcome came from the leaders of the Free Church where men like Andrew Bonar and Donald John Martin not only shared in the organisation of the Evangelists' missions but went flat out to reap the local harvests available within their own parish areas. Martin, for example, comments of his own experiences in Stornoway, 'The whole town was powerfully moved. In shop and office, on the street and in the field, the universal theme was Salvation.' There was, however, a notable and encouraging change in that the Established Church also took an interest in the activities of the Americans with no less a person than A. H. Charteris, Professor of Biblical Criticism in Edinburgh, visibly active in the first two campaigns.

Evaluating the long-term effects of these waves of revival is not easy; we can say, however, that the 1858 movement and, to an even greater extent, the Moody and Sankey visits, did leave many a worthwhile mark on Scottish Church life, both nationally and locally, which did not fade away for many years, if at all. These revivals did lead, in many parishes, to a real deepening of devotional life, with vigorous prayer meetings appearing in town and village alike. J. R. Fleming, for example, cites the claim made in the United Presbyterian Synod that one out of every four communicants in that entire Church was regularly present at monthly, fortnightly, or weekly prayer meetings as a direct result of the events of 1858. Alexander Whyte reports that the Moody and Sankey meetings so revitalised his prayer meetings in St. George's that they had to be held in the Church instead of, as formerly, in the Hall. As a further lasting result of the Americans' visits, there was sown the precious seed of co-operation between the Free Church and the Established Church which, in view of past hatreds, was remarkable beyond words. The ministers were at last coming to accept that they could work together on the basic problems confronting the Christian Church, and the congregations were beginning to open their eyes to those great elements they all had in common instead of fixing stolidly on those factors that still came in to divide. Most encouraging of all, the American-inspired wave of revival did couple a concern for salvation with positive efforts for man's more physical welfare. For instance, the provision of free breakfasts for those in need, increased mission work to the down-and-outs, and much of the Y.M.C.A. work sprang directly from this spiritual reawakening. Ministers and leading laymen alike were alive to the truth that the Gospel of Christ was not only concerned with the salvation of man's spiritual soul, but was of necessity concerned with the improvement of his physical and material condition.

It was in this regard that the earlier revivals can be said to have been too one-sided. Moody Stuart wrote in 1855, 'The one thing I care for is the salvation of the lost. It has long seemed to me that the only way in which I could do any good in the world was in the salvation of souls', and the same idea was frequently re-iterated by Milne and Burns in the earlier awakening in 1839. These preachers had little or no social message; the present life was for them simply a testing ground for fitness to enter the life to come; their preaching came nearer the sternness of John the Baptist than the love and compassion of Jesus Christ. These men preached to the emotions of their hearers and, successfully though they did this, the long-term results were not nearly so spectacular as those seen after the Moody and Sankey visits.

It was largely this appeal to the emotions that made several Presbyteries uneasy to the point that they instituted enquiries into the possible harmful effects of Burns, Milne and their associates on the people. Points of criticism included the lateness of the hour at which the evening meetings often finished, the subsequent breaching of the custom of having family worship in the home at a respectable hour each night, the extent to which young children were being caught up in the revivalists' frenzy, and the high emotional content of many of the evangelists' addresses which inevitably produced an equally emotional response from the worshippers. On this last point, there was in the nineteenth century a greater tradition of open unashamed weeping in Church, as a normal occurrence, than we ever expect today. There was the old woman in the Pleasance district of Edinburgh whose outlook was typical of many: speaking of Dr. Alexander Whyte, she said, 'There is no preacher whom I so willingly hear for he aye gars me greet.' Andrew Bonar, for his part, makes it abundantly clear in his diary that he would heartily respect such a sentiment, for there we find many comments of this sort, 'there were many tears in the Kirk on the Sabbath', while almost as frequently, we find him lamenting that such a thing happened all too rarely for his liking during his eighteen-year ministry in Collace, Perthshire. The north of Scotland, particularly, cultivated a more lachrymose tendency in worship than we would now countenance with any peace of mind. John Macrae, minister of Lochs in Lewis from 1857, often had to stop in the middle of his sermon because of the people's sobbing, while James Kennedy, minister of Aberfeldy Congregational Church in the 1820s, says that 'uniformly as he drew to a close, the place became a scene of weeping'. John Macdonald, the Apostle of the North, officiated at a never-to-be-forgotten communion service in Uig, Lewis, where 'there was a burst of universal sobbing and every face was astream with tears. The cloths of the communion tables were so wet with tears that they had to be wrung out.'

There is always the place for the true emotional response to the preaching of the love of God as the individual becomes aware of his own sinfulness and of God's redeeming mercy; but surely it can only be a personal response, with a corporate response of this kind scarcely something to be encouraged as a regular nightly routine; still less is it healthy for the same men and women continually to be reduced to this tearful state. For these reasons, then, we might feel that Burns and Milne considerably overdid the emotional content of their addresses day after day. Many are the examples that could be quoted; four will suffice to emphasise the pattern to which these revivalists worked. Burns reports one meeting in 1839 in these terms: 'At last their feelings became too strong for all ordinary restraints and broke forth simultaneously in weeping, wailing, tears and groans, intermingled with shouts of joy and praise from some of the people to God. Some were screaming in agony; others, and among these strong men, fell to the ground as if they had been dead.' Another Burns' 'special' is minuted thus: 'To me, looking from the pulpit, the whole body of the people seemed bathed in tears, old as well as young, men equally with women.' Even an audience composed of children was not spared: when McCheyne visited a school in St. George's Parish, Edinburgh, in 1839, he seemed satisfied that he had been able to preach to 'many weeping children'. The highlight for Burns, however, was clearly that momentous day when he dissolved the class barrier; 'Glory be to God; we had some of the *gentry* in tears.' We would not, in criticising this element in some phases of revival, play down the effects for good that came to Scotland and her churches through the always sincere labours of the nineteenth-century evangelists. We can, however, understand the reluctance of several Presbyteries, not only because of Moderate bias in their ranks, to give wholehearted approval to all that went on. It is also surprising that, in an age when religion was such a burning topic of general discussion, there were not more incidents like the one in Perth where a crowd of the local worthies, not in sympathy with the methods of Milne, registered their opposition in a pointless but very up-to-date way: 'The walls of Mr. Milne's Church, and other places, were scrawled over in chalk with figures and sentences, some ridiculous, some abusive and vile.'

Chapter 4

Woe is unto me if I preach not the Gospel

Since such factors as party allegiance, geographical situation, and the class-structure within parishes, could substantially influence a minister's approach to his daily work, it might seem highly unlikely that we could ever arrive at a generalised picture of the day-to-day pattern of life lived by the Scottish parish minister of the nineteenth century. Surely, we would think, regional variations alone – not to mention the vast changes that the passing years inevitably brought – would rule this out. But, if the extreme Evangelical and the ultra-conservative Moderate differed radically on many matters, the more conscientious on both sides did agree on their basic ministerial duty. A. J. Campbell listed the main items as 'preaching, catechising, visiting the sick, and taking oversight of the parish', a list substantially agreed on all sides. There is a common launching-pad; individuals' methods would vary; content and style of sermon would be very different; the ministers' visits might range in style from a dispensing of the merest gossip to the fulfilling of a high spiritual exercise; but these were accepted as fundamental inescapable duties for all ministers, Moderates, Evangelicals, or whatever, throughout the whole of the nineteenth century. From this starting point we try to determine the daily mode of life of the parish minister who was faithful to his duty and calling.

Recalling the 'slander' that ministers work only one day in seven, we begin here by looking at that portion of their time which they might spend in any week preparing for the labours of that day. In this, Erskine's quota of three addresses per Sunday can be accepted as the normal amount of such work confronting the parish minister at the beginning of the nineteenth century. Any attempt to calculate how many hours in the study would be needed to prepare for this work-load must recognise that there are certain important factors which would vary greatly with the individual. For example, the average duration of each finished address is very relevant, as is the mode in which it was delivered. If the minister were permitted to read his assembled thoughts verbatim, then his time within the study would surely be considerably briefer than if he were allowed only notes on the pulpit desk or, worse still, if he were expected to deliver his oration wholly from memory. We must also establish whether the ordinary worshippers considered it desirable for their preachers to have prepared their sermons down to the last jot and tittle, or whether they valued more highly the spontaneous address, but with, hopefully, the inspirational dictation of the Holy Spirit throughout. With all this said, however, there are always those who find preparation relatively easy and make rapid progress; there are those so fitted for public speaking that they have a fluency and spontaneity that, whatever their lack of specific preparation, always put in the shade their more plodding brethren.

Regarding the average length of a sermon, brevity within the context of the Communion was not considered a virtue. In the heat of revival W. C. Burns and the like could hold large congregations with sermons of several hours' duration. In one week's preaching tour in 1842, for instance, Burns kept the attention of 4000 hearers in Blair Atholl Churchyard for over five hours, and completed a further eight or nine memorable sermons, none of which was under three hours in length. Away from special events and exceptional circumstances, the normal parish minister did not expect to find his congregation clamouring for such protracted preaching as part of the weekly diet of worship, but even here there is much that must surprise modern ears. James Begg, whose main ministry was in Newington Free Church, Edinburgh, John Caird, who held charges in Edinburgh, Perthshire and Glasgow between 1847 and 1868, and John Macleod, minister of Govan Old Parish Church from 1875 to 1898, were three preachers whose normal weekly sermons were said never to be under the hour. Longer still were the sermons of Norman Macleod of the Barony (even in his special services for the poor), Murray McCheyne in St. Peter's, Dundee, and Dr. MacGregor of St. Cuthbert's, Edinburgh; all three regularly delivered sermons that stretched to an hour and a half. MacGregor in particular found it well-nigh impossible to be even tolerably brief. His biographer, Frances Balfour, says that his sermons were 'long at the first writing, and grew longer with revision'; MacGregor himself confesses that sheer length was 'a positive disease which I can't get the better of'; the minister of Crathie knew this failing in him just as surely as he knew Queen Victoria's marked preference for the shorter sermon. He therefore offered timely advice to MacGregor when he was due to preach in her presence: 'You are already aware that the three great secrets of success here are, Brevity, Brevity, Brevity.' The preacher's reply is not quoted; perhaps it was not very different from the response of Dr. Robertson who, when given the same advice prior to his first visit to the pulpit of Crathie, said, with all due reverence and concern, 'With God's help I will try to keep within the hour.'

While it is undeniable that these examples are all of preachers at the top of their profession, and possessed of a power and a personality that could capture and keep a person's interest more readily than could the average journeyman preacher doing his honest if not always inspired best, all the indications are that their sermons, in length, were within the limits laid down by established custom. In other words, the MacGregors and the McCheynes were not succumbing to the temptation to preach longer in the knowledge that their audiences found them compelling orators. Writing of the normal Sunday services in Scotland in the 1840s, Dr. Charles Warr says that the sermons were 'of at least an hour's duration', while Norman Maclean remarks that Cameron Lees in his three ministries was quite the exception in that his sermons never exceeded 20 minutes at a time when 'other ministers were reckoned by the hour'. It would seem, then, that for the greater part of the nineteenth century, Scotland's ministers were delivering each Sunday two sermons, ranging in length from sixty to ninety minutes, with, in addition, an expository lecture not markedly shorter. The historian, J. R. Fleming, pinpoints the early 1900s as the time when the traditional long sermon was replaced on a wide front by addresses of a mere thirty minutes' duration. Certainly in Crathie the move to curtail the preacher's loquacity was swift: where Queen Victoria had expressed a preference, her successor, King Edward, was unrelentingly specific. In a letter written in 1903, Cameron Lees remarks, 'The service at Crathie is very short and the preacher is not allowed to preach more than fifteen minutes; so whenever my time was up, I had to stop like a run-down clock.'

In passing, it is interesting to note that the normal parish service was further lengthened by the inclusion of prayers of quite breathtaking duration. Even discounting the indomitable John Milne of Perth who once uttered a prayer that extended to two hours and contributed to keeping his congregation in their places until 11 p.m., twenty and more minutes was quite normal for the main prayer at public worship week by week, while in not a few parishes, forty minutes was accepted by the worshippers – who, incidentally, had to stand throughout – as inevitable. It is not in envy at the thought that our ancestors could regularly do what today would be found almost as difficult as it would be distasteful, that we note two comments which suggest very firmly that our concept of prayer in public worship is rather different from that accepted one hundred and thirty or so years ago. James Brown, the biographer of James Eadie, minister of Cambridge Street U.P. Church in Glasgow, says of the main prayer in morning worship: 'From time immemorial it has been in Scotland famous for its great length and has in some cases degenerated into a review of all the events ecclesiastical, political, and social which have taken place during the week.' Echoing this opinion is Charles Warr, who, in his biography of Principal Caird, dismisses the prayers of the 1840s as 'almost invariably an interminable meander over the whole field of orthodoxy from the fall of man to the last judgment'. If we imagine that such protracted goings-on Sunday by Sunday could scarcely be popular, Donald John Martin quotes remarkable evidence to show that, with some at least, adequate length was the first essential ingredient in seemly worship. In the parish of Lochs in Lewis, 'a deputation once waited on their minister to say that a service of two hours was rather short – would he not give them three hours?' On the other hand, the cynic within us all can only appreciate the shrewd psychological approach of Dr. Robertson of Ellon who, wishing new gas heating installed in his church, promised that his services would not exceed one and a half hours if the people promptly contributed the necessary finance.

The average minister, then, had three hours or so of preaching looming before him each Sunday: only the gifted extempore orator could, we imagine, avoid being confined to his study for hours on end making himself ready for it. Making this more likely still was the fact that for much of the nineteenth century, the congregations almost universally expected their preachers to operate without any kind of visible notes in the pulpit to jog their memory; even a single sheet with the barest guiding headlines earned a man immediate disapproval and, as often as not, open and sharp rebuke. As the biographer of James Eadie says, 'In the estimation of the Scottish people, power of memory ranked highest among the requisite gifts of the occupant of a pulpit; the gallery watchers reported any paper that was disfiguring the fair page of the Bible; if there was any, this could blast even the very best reputations, particularly in rural areas.' Equally clear is the comment of Alexander Gerard in his lectures delivered to the students of Aberdeen University and published by his son in 1799: 'In most places it would be unnecessary to attempt proving that this exercise of memorising what is to be said is incumbent on a public speaker'; in further clarification, he quotes the words of Bishop Burnett, 'Reading is peculiar to this nation and is endured in no other.'

There were certainly ministers who did rely on notes to see them through; a few insisted in having the full script at hand in case of total memory collapse; some individuals dared to flaunt convention completely by reading word for word from their prepared manuscript. William Anderson, minister of John Street U.P. Church, Glasgow, in the 1840s, was one who championed the minister's right to read his sermons, while Thomas Chalmers, who held congregations spell-bound whereever he preached, read all his sermons and read them obviously and closely. Such was the genius and magnetic appeal of Chalmers that this deviation from orthodoxy was accepted by the worshipping public almost without adverse comment. Anderson, however, was less benevolently treated, for this was only one of several 'eccentricities' which he manifested and which disturbed both his congregation and his denomination. At a time when 'to speak of instrumental music in connection with divine service was regarded as little short of impiety', he was the bold and unrepentant author of 'an apology for the Organ'. When there were strict conventions as to what material could be incorporated into a sermon, he dared to quote Shakespeare from the pulpit as often as four times in the space of fourteen months, a 'crime' for which he was brought before his Presbytery.

The hope of the people in the pews was that their ministers would not be 'readers'; indeed, so unyielding were some congregations and office-bearers on this matter that not even the possibility of a complete memory failure on the part of the preacher swayed them in the slightest. The Rev. John Watson (the novelist Ian Maclaren) tells of his experience in Logiealmond, Perthshire, where he ministered from 1874 until 1877: an elder advised him early in his ministry there that should his memory fail during the sermon, he should simply give out a psalm until he had regathered his thoughts. Quite clearly, such a device, which to many of us today would be an acute source of embarrassment to all concerned, was infinitely to be preferred to the presence of even a single sheet of human manuscript in the pulpit. More entrenched still were the congregation of Duke Street Secession Church in Glasgow during the ministry of the Rev. Robert Muter which covered the period from 1800 to 1842: in his old age, he offered to return half of his stipend on condition that he was allowed to read his sermons instead of memorising them as previously. In inflationary days it is as hard to conceive of such a bribe being offered as it is to imagine it being refused. These, however, were very different times and Mr. Muter could make no impression on his people whatsoever: 'The stern anti-burgher guardians of the old customs refused to compromise'. Our sympathy must be with the controversial Edward Irving who, licensed in Kirkcaldy, 'signalised his first sermon by dropping it accidentally on the head of the precentor'.

In general, therefore, the ministers of the last century were committed to delivering around three hours of sermon material in each Sunday without the aid of any manuscript support. Fleming again traces a general change in attitude to the early 1900s by which time, he says, the use of notes and even straight reading was becoming more acceptable. It must appear doubly inevitable, then, even allowing for the spontaneous oratory of some and the incurable laziness of others, that the ordinary ministers would indeed have to spend many hours each week on the work of sermon preparation, and this is emphasised in biography after biography. Norman Macleod, for example, reckoned that it took him eight hours to write one sermon and four subsequent readings on the Saturday to memorise it. Principal Rainy told his father that seldom did a sermon cost him less than eleven hours in the study. James Begg regularly devoted each Wednesday and Thursday to the writing of his sermons, using Friday and Saturday to commit them to memory.

As always, there were those preachers who scorned such elaborate and time-consuming preparation: nor were they all within the ranks of the lazy and ineffective. Donald John Martin in Stornoway, for instance, frequently did not know an hour beforehand what his text would be, while the famous W. C. Burns would often stand silent in the pulpit for three or four minutes at the beginning of a sermon while flicking through the pages of the Bible in search of a suitable text from which to preach. If there were few who so trusted in the leading of the Holy Spirit, there were few whose trust was so amply justified. Norman Macfarlane very fairly comments, 'Congregations that were in suspense at the start were in an ecstasy of delight at the finish.' Less spectacular, perhaps, but still outwith the normal pattern, was John Macleod in Govan; his morning sermon was completed from start to finish on the Saturday afternoon, and his evening preparation was fully accomplished in one hour on the Sunday afternoon: that is, his sermon took him less time to prepare than it took to deliver.

Undoubtedly, however, Ian Maclaren paints what was the usual picture for most ministers when he says that for sermon preparation the Bible was regarded as a woodyard; the planks would be selected on the Tuesday after which they would be treated with saw and plane before finally being nailed together into a useful article of furniture. In practice, most men wrote out in full what they intended to say and then committed to memory all the salient points and as much of the precise phraseology as they felt desirable; further, it appears to have been regarded as allowable to have somewhere in the Church premises – perhaps in the vestry or on an out-of-sight ledge in the pulpit itself – a full script to be consulted in case of memory failure. At any event, it is fair to assert that some three full days in each week were set aside by the average clergyman of the nineteenth century for the task of sermon preparation.

There is perhaps no single reason for the emphasis the worshipper placed on the need for ministers to preach without notes being visible. Mrs. Oliphant, in her biography of Principal Tulloch of St. Andrews, suggests that a memorised sermon gave 'the pretence of extempore speaking', the thought being that the people would always prefer true extempore speaking but were realistic enough to know that few men were capable of it with any effectiveness or variety. There is certainly truth in this: the memorised sermon was seen as a compromise between the spontaneous dictation of the Holy Spirit and the cold detached work of the study desk. It is also relevant, however, to remember that in the Scottish Reformed Church, the sermon was seen as the centre and climax of any service of worship; this being so, there would be those who would feel most strongly that it should be carefully and prayerfully prepared to the point that it could be delivered fluently without recourse to reading. On this point, too, it is proper to note that congregations would utterly reject any preacher who dared deliver a sermon which properly belonged to someone else. It did not matter how good the sermon might be, or how relevant; the eminence of the original author was not considered; to preach a discourse that some other preacher had penned was to commit the unforgivable sin. Thomas Guthrie comments that any preacher found guilty of such behaviour was considered as 'guilty of a disgraceful, if not a dishonest transaction, of something far worse than smuggling, illicit distilling of whisky, or evading custom-house duties'.

On the other hand, it is interesting to discover that, while a minister could not borrow a fresh sermon from an illustrious colleague, and while he incurred immediate disapproval if he read his own new and diligently prepared material, he could, without inevitable censure, repeat the same sermon over and over again. Norman Macleod of the Barony, for example, freely admitted that he had preached one particular sermon on at least fifteen occasions including a service attended by Queen Victoria at Crathie. We ought not to be too surprised at this practice if the congregations in each case were different, but there are numerous examples where this was manifestly not so. John Cairns of Berwick, for instance, regularly undertook strenuous preaching tours, but if the physical strain was considerable, the intellectual effort needed was reduced by reason of the fact that he confined himself to just a few sermons which he rarely altered. Alexander MacEwen tells us that in the congregations where Cairns was well known a few smiles would be seen when a familiar text was announced; they were, however, 'smiles of pleased recognition', and 'plain people would boast how many times they had heard the same sermon from him and would indeed be rather sorry if the sermon was a new one'. This same minister was paid a handsome compliment by his office-bearers in that, in a time of serious overwork, they invited him to repeat previous series of lectures instead of preparing new ones. It is surely a mark of Cairns' ability and personality that the numbers attending the 'repeats' were not less than when they were first delivered. A similar situation existed in Liverpool during the ministry of John Watson. Robertson Nicoll tells of a member of Watson's Church who was absent from a particular evening service. The sermon that night was on 'the peace of God': she had heard it twice before, yet when she discovered what she had missed she was visibly upset; 'the entire family circle', she said, 'condoled with me in my loss'.

The realisation that there was this period in Scotland's past when those attending church took a vivid personal interest in all aspects of the sermon, both its content, its authorship, and its delivery, is encouraging: equally encouraging is the fact that all the evidence indicates that the vast majority of ministers took their time of preparation with a matching seriousness. Indeed, for many, the hours or days during which the sermons were hammered out were times of near total withdrawal from the world with the manse servant schooled in dealing politely but firmly with any who might interrupt unnecessarily. For example, one of the lay missionaries attached to John Cairns in Berwick reports that that preacher had a definite way of letting callers at this time know, without discourtesy, that he wished them to hasten their departure. More determined still was Alexander Somerville, Free Church minister in Anderston, Glasgow, from 1844 to 1847: it was on a Saturday that he undertook his sermon preparation and on that day each week he issued his servant with the same instruction, 'Now if the Queen calls today, tell her I am sorry I cannot see her till Monday.' For some men, the locked door of the study was not sanctuary enough. Thomas Guthrie retired to the Church Vestry, locking both Church and Vestry door against all comers; Dr. James MacGregor, while in Paisley High, regularly found refuge in the somewhat uncomfortable but very private Church steeple; Robert Finlayson, minister of Lochs in Lewis from 1831 to 1856, found his inspiration in a near-by cave; the Rev. Archibald Browning of Tillicoultry, who died in 1858, ensured his privacy rather more simply in that he much preferred to write his sermons in bed. The end result, however, justified to himself at least, this somewhat unorthodox approach: 'I always come to bed when I want to make a good sermon', he said.

Before leaving this aspect of the minister's week, there is one further observation which perhaps goes some way to explaining how our ministerial forefathers could, without recourse to notes, discourse on the Scriptures with a greater fluency and length than many of us today would find possible. There is a type of sermon in which it is almost easier to speak at length than it is to speak succinctly and briefly. We have grown accustomed to hearing sermons which are close-knit in construction, which are anchored firmly to the initial text, and in which the ideas flow onward in a logical and easily discernible pattern. It would have been difficult indeed for the average minister to prepare and memorise adequately three hours per week of this kind of disciplined material. Somewhat easier, however, would be the preparation of sermons which more resembled loosely connected rambles through a diversity of subjects and in which the text acted more as a starting point than an anchor. In such discourses, length is not in itself difficult to achieve; nor is the finished work necessarily difficult to memorise in a manner that will prevent the preacher 'sticking' in the pulpit. In such sermons, the preacher's favourite themes can, with wonderful regularity, be incorporated at some stage so that his words flow almost automatically; further, if several of his preconceived sermon headings get out of sequence, there is not the same damage done either to the construction of the whole or to the preacher's confidence. Many-headed sermons were in fact quite common for much of the nineteenth century; with each heading likely to involve several sections and sub-sections, it would take a very alert worshipper indeed to detect that point was not following point in the most logical pre-determined way. Boston of Ettrick, for instance, was the master of this type of sermon construction with one epic rising to eighty-six heads, another to seventy-six and many with well over fifty.

Equally, the nineteenth-century sermon, though obliged to start with a text from the Scriptures, knew little of our custom of making the subsequent address tie in with the theme of the text. When James Hamilton of Regent Square Church in London was a student, he wrote in his day-book in 1838, 'Some preachers use their text as a louping-on-stane; if by help of it they can only get mounted they do not care how far they go from it or if they ever see it again.' We have already referred to Charles Warr's comment that prayers could meander from the Fall to the Last Judgment; in the same essay he further alleged that the sermons were 'more often than not a repetition of the subject of the prayers on a more flamboyant and incomprehensible scale.' In that fictional masterpiece, 'The Annals of the Parish', John Galt might be thought to exaggerate in making his minister-hero, Micah Balwhidder, preach sixteen different sermons on a single text, 'Render to Caesar', but fact is stranger than fiction. Alexander Stewart, for instance, minister of Cromarty from 1824 to 1847, and the elected successor to Dr. Candlish in Free St. George's, Edinburgh, preached on the Red Heifer of the Book of Numbers 'for an endless series of Sundays and always with freshness'.

Such facts and comments may suggest that the burden of preparation laid on each minister week by week was rather less than we might, with our modern style of sermon, imagine. Nevertheless, preparation for the pulpit was in the last century almost universally regarded as the first and most important charge on a minister's time. Certainly Principal Tulloch of St. Andrews was in no doubt on this point: 'Sermon writing is a minister's first duty' was his expressed opinion; equally insistent was Professor W. G. Blaikie in the lectures he delivered to the students of New College, Edinburgh: 'Pastoral visitation, though so desirable, is a duty inferior to that of the pulpit and it is not to be allowed to interfere with its efficiency.' Most dogmatic of all, however, was Dr. Fairbairn of Newhaven who is quoted in these terms by Alexander Whyte, 'Prepare for the pulpit; above everything you do, prepare for the pulpit. Should it at any time stand with you between visiting a deathbed and preparing for the pulpit, prepare for the pulpit.' It would be sad to think that the ministers of the Gospel in any generation would ever carry out this last instruction to the letter, but the spirit of such advice was undoubtedly heeded by Scotland's ministers of the nineteenth century.

Chapter 5

Pure religion is this, to visit the fatherless and widows in their affliction

The other major recurring duty of every ministerial week was that of visiting the people in their homes. In the early part of the nineteenth century, this involved the minister in doing two things. As an invariable routine, he had to pay systematic catechetical visits to each household at least once in every year; in addition, he had to be ready, at any time, to pay a visit, or visits, to any home where there was illness or where death seemed imminent.

For the first fifty or sixty years of the last century, the catechetical visits continued to be of a formal and even of a severe nature. In these visits, the children of the household were examined, with every child of eight years of age and over being questioned individually. The words of the catechism had to be fully known even if they were not anything like fully understood; certain psalms and other passages of Scripture had to be recited without stumbling or prompting, and each child had to be able to repeat the particular text or passage which had been prescribed for him on the previous visit. Any hesitation or uncertainty brought immediate disgrace to the child and earned subsequent public rebuke for the parents.

Following the children's examination, the servants were subjected to much the same kind of enquiry, and the whole affair was concluded with a solemn admonition and address to all the members of the household, couched always in terms relating to their personal situation and duties. Just how searching the minister's questioning at this time could be, and how personal were the matters he was permitted to raise, is seen from the lectures delivered in Aberdeen University by Alexander Gerard. Published in 1799, these lectures formed the course of instruction which the Northern Divinity students would receive.

Speaking of the catechetical visits, Gerard says, 'The minister may inquire how the husband and wife behave to each other, give them directions for the practice of their several duties, point out to them faults of conduct; he may examine the masters and the servants, how they treat each other, he may inculcate on parents the obligation of taking care of the virtuous education of their children; he should recommend family religion, particularly the reading of the Scriptures.' Recognising that families frequently met together for such catechetical visits, Gerard offers this advice: 'In this case the minister has a fit opportunity of inquiring on what terms they live with one another; a minister may direct neighbours to keep an eye on the conduct of each other, to admonish each other privately whenever they find one another guilty of a fault, or wanting in any duty. By this means, they may be rendered useful monitors to each other.'

Even in those more religious days, the average household scarcely looked forward to such ministerial visitation, but it was extremely difficult to find any sure escape. Although the visits were regularly conducted during men's normal working hours, employers were expected to release their workers so that their annual spiritual examination could be timeously completed. Typical of many was Andrew Somerville, Secession minister in Dumbarton from 1830 to 1845; he had his elders distribute cards to those families shortly to be visited; each card stated clearly the precise day and hour at which Somerville would call. So successful was this method of working that he was able to say, 'I have gone over the whole congregation without a single member being absent, no master refusing the workman leave of absence for the short time that I was to be in the house.' Equally satisfactory was the response that John Cairns received in Berwick: again cards with full details were issued well in advance and 'the merchants and shopkeepers of the town never hesitated to let young people away from business in order that they might attend'. According to Principal Story, it was in the 1860s that the formal catechising of every household more and more gave way to the less severe, more informal type of visit. In the lowlands of Scotland particularly, the school-master-like tone and the rigid question-and-answer formula were forsaken as the ministers sought a more homely and appealing approach.

In the highlands, however, such a change was considerably later in coming. The Rev. Murdo Mackenzie was minister of Kilmallie Free Church from 1873 to 1887 and all through this period his diets of catechism remained true to the traditional pattern. His wife remarks with pride that 'at the catechising old and young were subjected to a most searching examination as to their historical and spiritual knowledge', adding, in a wonderfully descriptive phrase, that on these occasions her husband turned the adult mind inside-out and shook it. With such an approach frequently carrying over to the questioning of the children, it is little wonder that many a youngster dreaded the day of the catechising more than any other in the calendar. We can well understand how John Cairns could meet up with a boy of nine in the early 1870s who, though he could not hazard a guess as to the county in which he lived, could yet answer verbatim the question, 'What is man's chief end?'

So far as the lowlands were concerned, the visits of the minister that replaced the catechetical visits were not in any way of a light or frivolous nature. Indeed, they were always occasions of religious significance; invariably there was a time of prayer with the family and not infrequently there was a formal address as well. For all but the most pious, however, there was the blessing that these 'new' visits were generally much briefer than had been the traditional ones. Where a minister might question all and sundry for thirty or more minutes, he now moved on to the neighbouring household in half that time. In fact, in the majority of cases the ministers acted as if they had to adhere to a tight time-schedule, conducting their mini-services with clock-work but rarely undignified precision. Gossip, small-talk, secular triviality and the like were all firmly out-of-bounds. John Watson of Liverpool, for example, could be guaranteed to stay no more than fifteen minutes in each house, and he let it be clearly understood that in that time 'business was to be done and gossip left out'. John Macleod's assistants in Govan were under strict orders to complete not less than fifty house visits each in every week with the emphasis on the helpful word and relevant prayer. Alexander Whyte, who talked scathingly of pastors in the previous century who spent their visits 'cursing the weather and telling and hearing of the approaching marriages', never allowed himself the chance of falling into the same trap. He had, by nature, 'no small change of conversation' and he took care that none should develop, often staying in a house only long enough to repeat a verse of a hymn and say a prayer. It does in fact appear that many ministers, conscious of the great break with tradition that this style of visiting entailed, had a positive dread of secular conversation infiltrating what was an essentially serious occasion. On those unfortunate visits when John Caird in Errol found himself dragged into the 'interchange of banalities', he said that he experienced 'a thorough-going exhaustion' which the more normal, and mentally more arduous activities of visitation never caused him.

It is undeniable, however, that these new-style visits from the minister, brief and serious in tone though they were, were genuinely more popular with the people. They did successfully bring minister and people closer together; they suggested to the church members that their ministers were interested in them as individuals and not just as machines for storing and reciting the Scriptures and the catechism. The people felt pride in the fact that the minister, particularly if he were famous, had time to enter their homes and offer a personal prayer on their behalf. Indeed, to have a John or Norman Macleod utter a prayer in one's home was a matter to boast of for many a day; the hymn quoted by Whyte or the tracts left by Cameron Lees or Guthrie were for ever treasured. The ministers, too, found that they were able to be more genuinely homely when they could forget the age-old questions of the catechism, and many of them developed a technique which, while never devaluing the sacred nature of the visit, yet brought a glow to the heart of the working man. For instance, Alexander Whyte's visits, as we saw, could be very brief, but they were always personal; in one home he formally quoted a well-known verse of Scripture, and then, at the door, added 'Put that under your tongue and suck it like a sweetie.'

John Eadie was one of the pioneers in introducing a further measure of informality into the minister's house visit. Minister of Cambridge Street U.P. Church in Glasgow in the 1840s, he broke with the tradition of including a sermonette in each house, insisting only that each visit should conclude with prayer. More unorthodox still was Dr. Archibald Scott of St. George's,

Edinburgh, who, in his Pastoral Theology lectures to the Divinity students of Edinburgh late in the nineteenth century, went further in this direction than any clergyman of his prominence had hitherto dared: 'Avoid,' he said, 'ostentatiously talking religion, and the unctuous use of Scriptural phrases, but seek opportunity naturally to leave a word that may be remembered; do not think it necessary always to conduct a formal service; pray with the family if there is an opportunity, but do not think that the visit is wasted if there is none.' It is surely not proof of damaging secularism amongst today's parish ministers that we feel that Scott here wafted an encouraging breeze of common sense through the divinity halls. One who gave practical expression to this kind of advice – and that most acceptably and successfully – was George Morrison of Glasgow's Wellington Church. Inducted to that charge in 1902 as colleague to Dr. Black, his ministry properly belongs outwith the century which is our primary concern, but he was an outstanding example of the 'new pastor' who was opening up whole new areas of friendly contact between clergyman and communicant. Morrison is on record as saying, 'Pastoral work is the crown of my ministry': he averaged not less than 1000 visits each year, all of them methodically indexed for easy future reference: his congregation loved him as they had loved no other parish minister: and yet thirty or forty years earlier, the form and content of his house to house visits would have been thought quite unsatisfactory by ministerial colleagues and devout church members alike.

Morrison was fortunate in succeeding Dr. Black who, in this matter, was surprisingly 'modern' in his outlook. He had told his congregation, for example, that they should not 'expect their minister to conduct religious exercises at their homes as a regular thing', explaining with wonderful candour that conducting formal devotions nine or ten times a day could have a thoroughly deadening influence on even the most pious and other-worldly cleric. Thus, the congregation of Wellington was at least partially prepared for the coming of Morrison, who very soon decided that readings from the Scriptures and the repetition of prayers would normally be restricted to visits where there was illness or trouble of some kind. He admits readily, 'I often used to lose the happy freedom of Christian intercourse by the haunting thought that I must get a prayer offered before leaving.' For Morrison and the increasing number of ministers who thought in like terms, Christian fellowship and homely conversation were worthwhile ends in themselves. Above all, the aim of the routine house visit came to be that of getting-to-know and getting-to-be-known, and to this end Morrison copied the methods of Alexander Whyte and sent innumerable personal post cards to supplement his regular visits. Any promotion or success that any of his people gained was marked in this way; impending journeys, worrying news, bereavements even in far-off branches of the family, were likewise matters to warrant a card; indeed it often seemed that nothing could happen to any member of any associated family without Whyte and Morrison keeping track of it in this way.

Throughout the nineteenth century, the conscientious parish minister had his routine pastoral visitation to attend to, and, regardless of the type of visitation favoured, such work inevitably demanded many hours each week. James Begg, for example, devoted each Monday and Tuesday afternoon to this regular form of visitation. Others, such as Norman Macleod, Alexander Whyte, and Dr. Brown of Rose Street, stretched this to three afternoons in a week, while John Macleod, needing, as we saw, fewer hours than many for the business of sermon preparation, gave over almost every afternoon to meeting his people in their homes.

This being so, it might be possible to imagine that many a minister would regularly fight a battle within his mind as to which of his two main duties, preaching or visiting, was truly the more important. We can think of Morrison striving to complete his thousand visits in the year, and, at the same time, prepare adequately for the hundreds who queued up each week to hear him preach: we can picture Norman Macleod pacing up and down his study floor trying to commit to memory three hours of sermon material when he knew of many poor parishioners around the Barony Church whose day would be made by just a fleeting visit from him. We noted the advice of Principal Tulloch and Alexander Whyte to the effect that preaching was the more important duty; it would be possible now to produce an equally impressive array of spokesmen who might seem to exalt visiting more highly. From Alexander Gerard's lectures, for instance, we could quote this: 'The lower sort will reap more benefit from half an hour of private conversation, prudently conducted, than from the sermons of a whole year.' Robert Burns of Paisley similarly affirmed, 'Visiting is the very life-blood of a successful ministry: if we don't go to the people, they won't come to us.' Even more pointed was the opinion of John Macleod of Govan; for him, visiting was the 'primary duty of a faithful pastor'; 'nothing,' he said, 'could better promote the designs of the arch-enemy of human souls than that the shepherds of the Church should shut themselves up in their studies'.

In very few cases, however, does it appear that ministers consciously came to the point of deciding to relegate to a place of lesser importance either their sermon preparation or their routine visitation. In certain very busy town charges, there had to be a strict disciplining of time and work, but for the vast majority of men, these were seen as complementary rather than rival duties. They were allotted often an almost equal period of time in each week: if there was a difference in attitude or approach, it was that the hours of sermon preparation were much more barred against interruption than were those less formal hours when the minister sallied forth from his study to meet his people on their own ground.

As far as the congregations were concerned, however, it is possible, perhaps, to detect a change in attitude as the nineteenth century progressed. For the first fifty or sixty years of the century, the minister's arrival at one's house door was not an immediately attractive prospect as he came more to conduct an examination than to win friendship. In such circumstances, it is understandable if the minister's popularity depended on his abilities within the pulpit. With the changing pattern of house visits, however, the people's standard of judgment began to change also. Lord Sands, for example, in his biography of Dr. Archibald Scott, says, 'Among the humbler classes in Scotland generally, visitation of the people in their homes is the accepted gauge of ministerial efficiency.' Thomas Chalmers frequently claimed that 'a house-going minister makes for a Church-going people', a theory which more and more came to be proved in practice. Stevenson MacGill, ahead of his time in this as in so many things, said, 'The minister who is never seen, save once a week in the pulpit, can hardly expect to acquire or to keep a very strong hold of the affections of his people.'

Speaking at the Baptist Union in London in 1899, Robertson Nicoll, editor of the *British Weekly*, said, 'A minister is tempted to conclude that he will do his best work in visitation and organising; it is not so. If the preaching is not the life of the Churches, if it is dried up, everything will fail. The real test of a preacher's character is not the number of miles he walks or the number of meetings he addresses, but his diligence in doing the work for which God set him apart.' As the nineteenth century ended, the majority of Scotland's ministers would probably have agreed with that statement of Nicoll's; one could not be so sure about the members in the pews, however. They had grown to like the shorter, less flamboyant, sermon; they had begun to know their ministers as men like themselves, as men, called of God yet with the common touch; they had felt a new warmth in their relationship with their spiritual leaders as they shared a friendly supper at the fireside; more and more, the people of Scotland formed their estimate of the clergy away from the pulpit. Cameron Lees of St. Giles' carried a pedometer wherever he went. Even at the age of 75, he walked over 2000 miles in a year, many of these miles taking him to the homes of the poor in Edinburgh's slum tenements. The people loved him for it, and they loved his colleagues who likewise did not spare their legs or their time in moving among their parishioners.

Having seen something of the routine side of the minister's visits to the home, we turn now to his response to the needs of the sick and dying. When comparing the Moderates and the Evangelicals, Sir Henry Moncreiff Wellwood said, 'Visitation of the sick and dying is a labour of perpetual recurrence and it is in no country of Christendom more faithfully attended to than in Scotland.' Referring directly as it does to that vexed period in the history of our Church when it is easy on a superficial reading to be depressed about the calibre of the ordained ministry, it is added encouragement to read such a glowing tribute and to find abundant proof of its honesty and accuracy; indeed, no matter where we look in the nineteenth century as a whole, all the evidence points to the fact that the honest parish minister was extremely diligent in this vital part of his ministry.

For instance, Murray McCheyne, himself almost continually in ill-health, visited anyone who was sick as often as half a dozen times in the space of a couple of days, continuing such devoted attention until the patient either recovered or died. John Milne in Perth, too, visited all his invalids at least once each day and if he was unable to call in person, he invariably sent a note or a card or a tract, all with pencilled texts for the invalid or his relatives to look up. So seriously did William Robertson of Irvine Secession Church take this responsibility that he willingly visited the sick whenever they were in most need of comfort or whenever they were normally most alert and widest awake; in this way, midnight visits were no novelty to him, nor were they regarded as an inconvenience.

Similarly, mere distance was not seen as a barrier to duty. Norman Macleod tells of ministers in the north of Scotland who would, without grumbling, walk sixteen or more miles to visit one parishioner who was sick. James Begg, at the age of 72, journeyed from Edinburgh to Moffat to call personally on one of his flock who had taken ill while there on holiday. On a similar errand, Thomas Guthrie crossed the Border into England on one occasion. Now all this would in itself be most praiseworthy, but such visits were not simply seen as occasions for conducting comforting and reassuring religious devotions at the bedside. Even in the days when the routine ministerial visit was concerned with rehearsing the catechism and little else, the minister was at pains, wherever possible, to cater for the physical needs of those temporarily laid aside by illness. For some, this meant carrying in buckets of coal, chopping firewood, cooking a meal, or seeing to the delivery of necessary household provisions. J. P. Struthers of Greenock, for example, tells with obvious pleasure that he managed to make a plate of porridge to the satisfaction of his oldest member who was confined to bed.

For others, however, their acts of mercy on these occasions showed a devotion which in some cases amounted to real heroism. Typhus and cholera were all too frequent visitors to our country during the last century, and always they brought widespread suffering and large numbers of deaths. In the typhus epidemic in Glasgow in 1865, for instance, over 1100 people died. In such circumstances, many ministers became not only pastors but nurses and even doctors. Skilled medical attention was scarce in many places; the people lacked the knowledge and the ability to take the necessary precautions to prevent the spread of infection, and, most important, there was such a fear of these diseases that, once a house became infected, no outsider would cross its door. In short, many a minister went where no one else would go and did what no one else would do. In Arbirlot, Thomas Guthrie was the only person in the epidemic of 1834 who was prepared to enter infected houses and care for the sick; John Milne was similarly on his own in this work in Perth, while John Eadie in Glasgow had it as his invariable rule that he would visit all infected homes within his parish whether he was needed as a 'nurse' or not. It was the logical, if somewhat grisly, outcome of such devotion that ministers found themselves in the role of undertakers. Norman Macleod's father in Torrance, and the elder Story in Rosneath were two who on occasion had to dress and coffin the bodies of those who died of fever and whose relatives, for fear of infection, would not go near.

Many of the most popular ministers in the towns included in their parish magazines, and even in their Sunday services, practical advice on hygiene and on steps to beat infection. Norman Macleod included in his special evening services for the poor purely secular advice of this sort; Principal Story devoted part of the Rosneath magazine to elementary medical hints; and James Begg and others toured the country giving lectures under the auspices of such bodies as 'The Glasgow Auxiliary of the London Ladies Sanitary Association'. It was a further sign of ministerial determination to contribute positively to the fight to eliminate the threat of such epidemics that local Medical Officers of Health regularly found in parish ministers their staunchest allies in publicising programmes of health education. Dr. MacGregor of Glasgow's Tron Church, and Alexander Somerville of Anderston were two who organised teams from their congregations to 'preach the unknown doctrines of fresh air, pure water, and whitewash' as part of Glasgow's efforts to combat cholera in the outbreak of 1866; and many others of their colleagues throughout Scotland saw such action as a valid part of their ministry to the sick.

In the early part of the nineteenth century, particularly in rural areas, some ministers actually set out to care medically for their people as an everyday practice and quite unconnected with any specific emergency. Some, like Thomas Guthrie in Arbirlot in the 1830s, simply kept a medicine chest in the manse and acted as dispensers in the absence of any qualified person; Norman Macleod's grandfather in Morven had done the same; and until as late as the 1850s there were parishes – Garrabost for example – which were still dependent on the manses for their medical supplies. Others, like Patrick Forbes of Bonharm, acted as district vaccinators, although this practice did not long survive into the century. For the first forty or more years of the century, however, there were parish ministers who, in addition to their normal duties, were acting as General Medical Practitioners for their parish areas. Mr. Kirkwood in Holywood, Dumfries, was famous for miles around in the 1830s as a good, if rather inadequately trained, doctor; at the same time, the people of Bellshill in Lanarkshire were entrusting their health to John Jamieson, the Relief Church minister, who had attended a few medical classes in his youth, while in Aberdeen, Dr. Thomson, minister of St. Clement's Church until his death in 1838, managed to treble an already generous stipend by caring for the sick in body as zealously as he could ever care for the sick in soul. In fairness to Dr. Thomson, he was a fully qualified doctor and, by all accounts, an exceptionally skilful one. It is interesting to note in passing that there are comparatively few instances of ministers being involved in the kindred spheres of dentistry and veterinary medicine. Henry Duncan in Ruthwell was, to his complete satisfaction, his own dentist, but he declined to try his skills on anyone else; and there was a minister near Cameron Lees in Strathconan whose main area of usefulness would appear to have been among the four-legged members of his parish: 'As a minister he was of no account, but as a cow doctor he was a man greatly esteemed and valued not only in his own but in neighbouring parishes.' These apart, however, ministerial examples of these attributes are decidedly few.

From all this it becomes clear that Scotland's ministers, throughout the nineteenth century, were regular visitors to the homes of their people. If a man remained healthy and attended Church week by week, he could look to see his minister in his home at least once a year when the visit would have a distinctly religious flavour; if a person was taken ill, he could expect his minister not only to call with unflagging regularity but to attend willingly to his different needs both spiritual and material; if a Church member was absent from his pew without known reason, he could almost guarantee that the preacher would make a prompt call to investigate. John Milne in Perth devoted each Sunday evening to this duty, giving, wherever possible, a résumé of the sermons that the absentee had missed; others, like Andrew Bonar in Finnieston and Alexander Campbell in Irvine Secession Church, waited until the Monday or Tuesday, but their thoroughness was no less complete.

The bond between minister and people was kept strong. The minister was anxious to keep his people in the straight and narrow, and the various house visits contributed greatly to this; the people could not but admire and even love a man who, if necessary, would work round the clock on their behalf and face real personal danger for their welfare. Alexander MacEwen is surely right when he says, in his biography of Cairns of Berwick, that the unflagging regularity with which ministers visited their people has, more than anything else, 'given the clergy of Scotland a hold upon the Scottish people'.

Chapter 6

Suffer the little children to come unto me

Having seen something of the formal link that existed between minister and child as a result of the regular catechetical examination, we look now at the other common points of contact in this relationship. For much of the nineteenth century, the principal meeting-point was in and through the day-schools, for, until the State took full responsibility for education in 1872, the schools in Scotland were Church-controlled, the supervision of their work being entrusted to Presbyteries and parish ministers. Thus conscientious clergymen had ready access – daily if they wished – to the young people in their parishes. In addition, many of the teachers were divinity students en route to ordination by way of the 'partial attendance' provision referred to earlier, while others of the teaching fraternity were 'stickit' ministers who, in a market over-supplied with qualified clergymen, had been unable to obtain a parish. In normal circumstances the bond between Church and School could not but be strong, with minister and teacher at one in efforts to impart the essentials of the Christian Gospel to the scholars. In many parishes the tie-up between Church and School was completed with the appointment, for a small salary, of the school-master as session clerk, precentor, and, on occasion, district catechist. 'The minor canon in the parish cathedral' is how Norman Macleod very aptly described such a schoolmaster.

There is considerable doubt, however, as to how seriously many of the ministers, and even Presbyteries, took their duties of school supervision. There were those, with a keen interest in the work, who spent many hours in the schools among the children, but perhaps they hardly constituted a majority of the clergy. In the parish of Eastwood near Glasgow, Stevenson MacGill, who ministered there from 1790 to 1797, took great pains to superintend the various schools in his parish, 'not satisfying himself with the annual and perhaps formal inspection of them by the members of the Presbytery'. Dr. James MacGregor, minister of Paisley High from 1855 to 1862, likewise took this side of his work seriously and one list of his labours shows that he visited no fewer than eighteen schools in his efforts at adequate superintendence. Earlier in the century, Henry Duncan of Ruthwell had undertaken more than any Presbytery could ever have asked, spending several hours in the parish school each week in an attempt to win the friendship and confidence of the youngsters.

It is, however, undeniable that in many places, the duties of supervision were regarded more lightly. For example, we can quote the testimony of Thomas Guthrie who was inducted to the parish of Arbirlot near Arbroath in 1830: 'I was seven years in Arbirlot, and while I believe I was just as attentive as my neighbours, I do not recollect of being three times in the parish school, though it was next door to me, except on those occasions once a year when the Presbytery committee came to examine the school. The truth is, Presbyterial supervision was very much a decent sham; to sit for weary hours hearing a-b ab, b-o bo, was the dreichest business I ever had to do with, and well do I remember to have seen how often the watches were pulled out to see how time went; and the truth is that if the "diet of examination" had not been followed by another kind of diet in the Manse – a committee dinner and a sociable crack with the brethren – there would have been very few at the diet of examination.'

We must be cautious, then, in assuming that school work would occupy much of a minister's normal week, but we could never underestimate the effects on the children of the close links, however formalised some may have become, between their church and their school, and we can well understand the decision of the Free Church to erect their own schools to preserve for their children the precious harmony between these two great centres of early training. In all the schools, the Bible was the main text book, something that continued for some years even after the State take-over in 1872, and suitable parts of the Book of Proverbs formed many a first reading book. As the historian J. R. Fleming says, 'No child could leave school without the deep-rooted conviction that the Bible was the greatest book in the world'. Even where the teacher was neither a divinity student nor a 'stickit' minister, he had to subscribe to the same Confession of Faith as had the ministers at their ordination. Inevitably, some of the Church's influence was lost following the events of 1872, but, generally speaking, ministers had little difficulty in gaining a position on the new city and parish school boards where they could be as active as their interests determined.

We move now to the more informal areas of contact between minister and child in an attempt to discover to what extent the minister and the Church sought to capture the lasting interest of those who in years to come would constitute the congregations. For the first fifty or so years of the nineteenth century, the average Sunday service in Scotland did not contain anything which could today be called a 'children's address'; nor were specially designed family services by any means common. For instance we possess only one manuscript for a children's sermon from the pen of Thomas Guthrie, who died in 1873; and yet from his work in his Ragged Schools and special Sunday Schools he was passionately concerned for the spiritual and physical welfare of the children in his Edinburgh parish. The simple fact is that within the established pattern of public worship, there was no place allotted to any item specially for the children. Even such as Andrew Bonar, minister at Finnieston, Glasgow, until his death in 1892, and Alexander Whyte, who finally resigned his charge of St. George's, Edinburgh, in 1916, who both loved children around them, considered that three or four children's sermons a year – delivered usually the Sunday following Communion – were sufficient.

In partial explanation, through the catechetical examinations the minister could satisfy himself that the children were being adequately instructed in the rudiments of the faith. Furthermore, for much of the last century, the home was expected to provide sound elementary teaching of the Christian religion, and to our forefathers' credit, this was fairly conscientiously done, so that much of what we have to do today in the Sunday school and in the Children's Address was being more effectively done round the home fireside. The result was that young people did enter the family pew on a Sunday much better informed than do their twentieth-century counterparts. To this extent the ministers did not need to pay the specific attention to the young people within the normal services that they do today.

This, however, is not the whole story. The Church Service in Scotland was, by tradition, an entirely solemn occasion; there was little room in it for the lighter touch which an address to children so often requires. Likewise, many of the ministers were themselves solemn and scholarly to the point that they lacked the ability to come down to earth in such an atmosphere and communicate satisfactorily with the young mind. Out of the pulpit, many of these men could and did unbend and become great favourites with the children, but their interpretation of the dignity of their sacred office, and the traditional mood of public worship, prevented, for long, any intrusion into the Sunday service of an address that might appeal specially to children. For much of the century, too, there was no need to 'attract' young people to Church with items tailor-made for them; the influence of the Church was such that their parents saw to it that they duly attended week by week.

As the century progressed, however, changes did come and the young worshipper began to be recognised in his own right. One of the pioneers was James Robertson, minister of Newington U.P. Church from 1848; he was one of the first to include in each of his morning services a part specially for the children, and his biographer claims that the success with which he incorporated this into the accepted framework of worship did a great deal to make this practice more general. Robertson also introduced periodic services where everything was planned to appeal to the younger people, and he always made sure that visiting preachers knew that in his church this age group was not to be forgotten. In a typical letter to one brother minister who was to occupy his pulpit, he said, 'Please remember to bring a handful of tender grass for the lambs.'

Before such practice became widespread, various experiments had been tried to make sure that the younger worshipper took as much as possible from the Sunday service. Some ministers took ten or fifteen minutes immediately following the morning service to ask the children present some questions on the theme and development of the morning's sermon; in this way, any point which had been above their heads could be simplified. Alexander Moody Stuart, inducted to St. Luke's, Edinburgh, in 1837, used this approach with considerable success, and indeed it is not hard to see that the devout parents also derived real help from this question and answer sequence. Rather more common, however, was the gradual appearance of a third Sunday service designed first and foremost for young people. Dr. Archibald Scott in St. George's held such a service on the first afternoon of each month and personally derived as much real pleasure from it as did the many children who attended. Archibald Charteris, coming to Glasgow's Park Church in 1863, conducted such a service each Sunday afternoon at 1 o'clock, that is, in between his regular 'adult' services; while in Govan, John Macleod replaced his afternoon service with an evening one but used the afternoon hour for weekly services for the youth of the parish. Interesting, too, was the system adopted in Cowcaddens Free Church, Glasgow, by William Ross who ministered there from 1883 to the end of the century. At each morning service, the pews in the centre area of the Church were boldly labelled 'Children only', and during the second or third hymn each week, the children filed in from the Hall to occupy these places. 'The next item in the service was the recitation of the text for the day by a selected number of the boys and girls called on by name from the pulpit.' This was followed by an address to the children and the whole institution was called the 'Children's Church Society'.

Amid this chronicle of change, two facts surely emerge: it is good to see Scotland's ministers more willing to help the young mind grapple with the complexities of the Christian faith; it is also immensely encouraging to read of children now anxious to attend Sunday service in that it contained positive elements that they could truly enjoy. Natural respect for their ministers, instilled in them from their very earliest days, was thus heightened by a bond of affection which, rightly handled, would have more than compensated for the weakening of the iron hand of the catechism and the Church-controlled school. One of Alexander Whyte's assistants, in St. George's, was George Morrison, later minister of Glasgow's Wellington Church. His sermons to the children proved so popular that many of the children from St. George's begged to be allowed to spend their summer holidays in Thurso – the town where Morrison took up his first charge in 1894 – so that they might hear more of them.

Today, we expect our ministers to be actively involved in the work of Sunday schools and Bible classes: without doubt, this is a most valuable point of contact with the youngsters, but it was only in the course of the nineteenth century that this branch of the Church's work came to be established on anything like a large scale. We have already remarked that Jupiter Carlyle in Inveresk was ahead of his time in introducing Sunday schools in 1790 when many of his colleagues regarded them as 'nurseries of sedition'; in fact, the General Assembly of 1799 went rather further and denounced such gatherings utterly, the reasoning being that Sunday schools allowed untrained teachers to teach impressionable minds the basics of the faith, thus weakening the authority of the ministers and lessening the lazier parents' sense of responsibility for maintaining religion within the home and the family circle. Elsewhere, many a kirk session specifically spoke and acted against the formation of Sunday schools, even where their ministers might have been persuaded to give them a try, while the Rev. Alexander Campbell of Irvine and those like him were prepared to institute such schools as long as they did not meet on Sundays. The whole idea of groups of probably noisy children meeting in a hall seemed a definite 'disturbance of the day of hallowed rest', with the result that many parishes introduced Saturday church schools which, however approved by parents and elders, were heartily disliked by the children who thus saw their one totally free day being eaten up with an activity that seemed to combine the strict discipline of both school and church.

Despite the fact that Sunday schools are said to have begun in Brechin with the Rev. Mr. Blair as early as 1760, it was not until at least the 1830s that they began to be regarded as normal and acceptable. Initially, most of the schools were taught by ministers and any divinity students or stickit ministers they could enrol, but soon responsible laymen were introduced into this sphere of work. It is to be regretted if ministers felt it necessary to inaugurate Sunday schools because they saw the religious training of the home becoming more and more haphazard, but without a doubt these new organisations benefited many more than just the youngsters who came to attend them. One clear bonus to the Church as a whole was the new level of involvement of the laity who, hitherto, had been too much neglected within the ecclesiastical framework of Scotland. Kirk Sessions tended to be small, with the result that talented men and women were condemned to a purely passive role in the work and witness of the Church – something which could not be for the greater good of the Church. Clearly, however, it was the children who were most affected by these new Sunday meetings. We saw enough of what town housing was like to know that the children were better elsewhere during the long hours of a Sunday, and yet once they ventured out of doors, there was virtually nothing they could do. Public parks and shops alike were closed: indeed, not even an open shop window could be found to brighten the scene. But, until the Forbes Mackenzie Act of 1854, the public houses were open, so that the Sunday streets were not just drab for the youngsters: they were at times positively unsafe. It is little wonder that the Sunday schools proved so popular. Robert Burns in Paisley, for example, counted over 1000 in his Sunday school in the 1830s, while Norman Macleod in the Barony regularly had more than 1400 scholars. It is both exciting and a trifle pathetic to read in the Baird Lectures delivered by Archibald Charteris in 1887 that there were numbers of children who each week set out to attend as many Sunday schools as was possible. By going the rounds of those that met at different times, some were apparently able and eager to attend four or five each Sunday: he even manages to cite the case of one breathless individual who crammed in an appearance at no less than seven Sunday schools each week.

A regular feature of the Church's work among young people today is the wide availability of week-night organisations and activities specifically geared to their interests. Though the minister may not be directly in charge, he has, because they meet usually in Church premises, open access to the youngsters who share in them. This, however, is yet again a fairly modern development. In the early part of the nineteenth century, it would have been genuinely difficult for ministers to establish much in the way of week-night gatherings for young people. Church Halls were not plentiful prior to the 1840s, and even young children of nine or ten years of age had to work long hours in factories: a working day of eleven hours was regularly demanded of them, with a reduction to nine hours on Saturdays. Their main need of an evening was for adequate sleep. Donald

Macleod, for instance, was made very aware of this problem in his Linlithgow parish. Inducted to that charge in 1862, he wished to provide classes to teach the children reading and writing. From a very early age, however, the children of that area were employed in 'closing' boots and shoes with the result that Macleod found them so tired at night that no real progress could be made by way of regular night schools. He therefore took the bold step of including such training in his Sunday morning classes.

Elsewhere, the minister's classes for young men and women, to which we have already made some reference, were the nearest the Churches came early in the century to having any kind of activity for younger age groups outwith the normal services. Even accepting that 'young' was interpreted liberally, many of these series of classes were outstandingly popular: Dr. Alexander Whyte regularly had 600 men at his weekly lectures, with an almost similar number crowding into his meetings for women. In the last quarter of the century, however, something like our present-day pattern of week-night activities began to take shape. At some of these developments we shall have cause to look later: in the meantime, it is sufficient to note that in a busy church, such as Govan Old Parish was in the ministry of John Macleod from 1875 to 1898, a great deal was happening in the formerly quiet period of Monday to Saturday: that congregation had at that time three Sunday schools, a daily service, four weekly instruction classes, a system of house-to-house collectors, district visitors, a mother's meeting, a church choir and a junior choir, a Dorcas Society, a young man's literary association, professionally-taught classes in cooking and domestic economy, a Boys' Brigade Company, Girls' Clubs, and an Evangelistic Association. There, as elsewhere, however, the detailed leadership of this new wave of activity was in the hands of the laymen, with the minister the interested friend and adviser in the wings.

To return to what the average minister did to establish friendly relationships with the young people of his parish, there were wide differences of approach on the part of the ministers. There were those who were all too frivolous in their attempts to amuse the children: Alexander Carlyle tells of two ministers from Dumfriesshire who 'had a great turn for fun and buffoonery and wore their wigs back to front and made faces to divert the children in the middle of a serious discourse'. Happily very few like this appear in the pages of Church history, even although Carlyle goes on to assure us that they were none the less 'pious and orthodox clergymen'. Rather more common, perhaps, particularly in the stern north, were those ministers who went quite to the other extreme and refused to unbend at all, even when they were outwith their sacred duties. Typical of this austere brigade was John Macrae, inducted to the parish of Lochs in Lewis in 1857. His adult congregation 'had a fear of him', and 'children fled hurry scurry at the sight of him'. Likewise, the young people in Stornoway in the 1850s and 1860s fled from the approach of the Rev. Peter Maclean who, we are told, 'breathed an air of stern sanctity as if he had been sleeping with John the Baptist'.

Fortunately more and more of Scotland's ministers, as the nineteenth century wore on, found a satisfactory middle way between these two extremes. They did not descend to any unorthodox behaviour that would have lessened the children's respect for the clerical office, but they did manage to recapture, when appropriate, a childlike appreciation of what young folk enjoyed in life. Robert Candlish joined enthusiastically in some of their games, making sure that he knew the rules so that his enjoyment was not less than theirs; Principal Rainy took time each week to read the *Boy's Own Paper* in order that he might be able to converse with his own and other people's children on topics familiar to them. (Incidentally, his leisure reading also extended to various women's journals where he laboured diligently in discovering and understanding latest trends in women's fashion: his idea always was to be able to talk with all sorts and conditions of the people on subjects away from his own narrow theological sphere, so that they in turn might more readily listen to him when he did turn to speak on matters pertaining to his calling.) John Milne and Cameron Lees were two of many who usually carried in their pockets a supply of booklets and tracts especially suitable for children; these they gave to any youngster to whom they spoke. In many places, however, this 'what's-in-my-pocket' approach operated on even more basic lines, in that the ministers, going their parish rounds, came to be known as reliable suppliers of fruit and sweets and even of pocket money. William Dunn, minister of Cardross from 1838 to 1881, was a great favourite as his coat-tail pocket 'seemed to have an inexhaustible supply of red apples'; Dr. Archibald Scott of St. George's, who could wherever necessary be rather stern, nevertheless disbursed sweets very freely to children whom he met, a thoroughly engaging habit which, says his biographer Lord Sands, was 'his only levity'.

Elsewhere, special occasions and circumstances were frequently marked by ministers with gifts for their young parishioners. Each New Year in Rosneath the younger Story invited all the children of the Sunday school to the manse where they were given oranges and cakes, while in Greenock, J. P. Struthers never visited any child in hospital without taking him a 'poke' of sweets. Most consistently generous, however, was the remarkable John Milne in Perth. We noted that he handed out booklets in plenty, but accompanying the reading material was often the opportunity of considerable financial reward for the fortunate youngster: 'He used frequently to promise children sixpence or a shilling if they could learn a certain Psalm or Chapter and repeat it to him. His card would frequently be handed in to Mrs. Milne by some boy with this pencilled on it: "Give the bearer sixpence if he repeats the 53rd of Isaiah." ' For all that Milne was the great Evangelical orator, he had both a genuine love of children and the ability to get on their level. An unnamed admirer writes, 'He used to be so kind to our children one winter, giving them slides.' Horatius Bonar pays this tribute which surely would be a justifiable cause for pride in any minister who was worthy of it, 'He was very fond of children, and almost every child in Perth knew him. Constantly, in the street, he would stop to play ball with one, or throw the skipping rope with another.'

The children of Scotland entered the twentieth century in a more privileged position, relative to the Church, than had their predecessors a hundred years before. Their distinctive spiritual needs were better understood and more fully met; concerned laymen were being encouraged to expand their leisure pursuits under the umbrella of the Church's supervision; the ministers were open to view them as a separate group within society who had a language, an intellect, and interests of their own.

Chapter 7

Let your light so shine before men that they may see your good works

It is now time to look at our nineteenth-century minister in his more distinctly public role, at those agencies and institutions which, while set up for the benefit of the whole community, were organised and administered solely or largely by the minister, and at the minister's position relative to the main secular bodies within his parish.

The Savings Bank movement in Britain owes its origin to clergymen. In England, the man responsible was the Rev. Joseph Smith of Wendover: in Scotland, the genius was the Rev. Henry Duncan, minister of Ruthwell near Dumfries. First hearing of Savings Banks in Germany, Duncan published articles praising their merits in the *Dumfries and Galloway Courier*, the paper which he edited, and his Ruthwell Bank opened in May, 1810. Duncan was no mere titular head of his bank; he acted most ably as its actuary until his death; he himself gave sound advice and practical help to those, many of them parish ministers, who were interested in opening similar banks in their own areas; and in 1819 and 1835 he went south to London to assist the Members of Parliament in drafting the Parliamentary Bills which were to govern Scotland's Savings Banks. Much of the popularity of these new banks rested on the fact that they provided the ordinary working people with the opportunity of saving week by week such small sums of money as they were able to put aside from their wages. The existing banks did not accept deposits of less than £10, whereas Duncan's aim was that a shilling or less might be lodged at any time.

Without a doubt, these new banks met a genuine need, and their progress was both rapid and dramatic. Just eight years after the Ruthwell opening, there were, outside of Glasgow and Edinburgh, 130 popular Savings Banks in Scotland with about a thousand members and £30,000 in deposits. Many were established by parish ministers, with not a few operating directly from the manse as the bank office. For instance, Robert Lundie of Kelso – a direct disciple of Duncan – the younger Story in Rosneath, Charteris in Edinburgh's Tolbooth Kirk, Norman Macleod in the Barony – his was one of the first congregational penny savings banks in Glasgow – William Hamilton in Strathblane, and Thomas Guthrie in Arbirlot, are just a few of the famous 'finance ministers'. Guthrie's autobiography shows very clearly how a manse bank operated: 'I was the entire manager, giving money out only on a Saturday morning, and that only on a week or fortnight's notice, but receiving it in the shape of a shilling, the lowest deposit, at any time and any day, Sunday, of course, excepted.' He further adds, 'The success of the bank and library I attribute very much to this, that I myself managed them. They were of great service by bringing me into familiar and frequent and kindly contact with the people. They trusted me, where they would not others, with a knowledge of their money affairs. The lads and lasses liked that their minister should see that they were economical and self-denying and thriving even in this world and that they should rise in his good opinion.'

This was one aspect of its work which the Church could neither wish nor expect to retain indefinitely. As it became obvious that a national network of savings banks was desirable, so independent banks, with professional staff and security-conscious offices, inevitably sprang up. (In fairness to Guthrie, however, he was himself a trained banker, having worked for two years in the bank at Brechin in the period between being licensed and receiving the call to Arbirlot.) The Post Office Savings Bank also made its appearance and prospered, even although the younger Story complained that it was 'strangled with red tape'. All credit to the ministers, however, not only for seeing the need that existed, but for endeavouring, surprisingly capably, to meet it.

Until the relevant Parliamentary Act of 1845, the relief of the poor in Scotland 'rested in the hands of the Kirk Session, supported by the heritors in country parishes and by the magistrates in the burghs'. The Kirk Session financed this work from Sunday collections taken at the church door, from special gifts from wealthy philanthropists in the parish, from mortifications, and from sundry odd fees and fines. The money available from these sources, however, was rarely large, and in times of bad harvests or unemployment, kirk sessions were unable to offer the aid their people needed: in Ruthwell, for example, the average annual income for the poor fund was just £25. There was, therefore, a strong movement as the nineteenth century progressed in favour of a system of compulsory legal assessments to make available poor relief on a realistic scale. After much initial opposition, the Church as a whole turned in favour of this idea, particularly in the rapidly expanding towns, where harassed kirk sessions could not cope with the queues of folk clamouring for assistance. Furthermore, the Disruption of 1843 created around 500 sessions who needed every penny to erect buildings and pay salaries, and, at the same time, left an almost like number of churches and sessions, so depleted in personnel, in finance, and in morale, that they could neither provide adequately for their own poor nor think to cast a kindly eye towards their former colleagues who had betrayed them in 'going out' to the Free Church.

The voluntary system of poor relief, then, was manifestly inefficient when the Act of 1845 established nationally a system of legal assessments and took the care of the poor out of the hands of the local churches. On the whole, the churches were satisfied that the welfare of the poor was now better safeguarded, and they were content in the knowledge that elders, representing their sessions, were afforded, as of right, places on the new parochial boards for poor relief. There were those ministers, however, who remained opposed to the new set-up. Duncan in Ruthwell cherished the hope that, by saving regularly in the new savings banks, the people of Scotland would be able to help themselves through any time of hardship. Thomas Chalmers, too, was an implacable foe of state charity, and under his dynamic leadership his congregation proved that the voluntary system could indeed work wonders. The area around St. John's Church in the 1820s was not prosperous, but Chalmers and his dedicated laymen so managed the poor fund that it was adequate to the calls made upon it. In the very different rural setting, Duncan is equally to be admired. He established his bank, he reconstituted an earlier Friendly Society to provide assistance in time of accident, disease, or bereavement, and, as we have already noted, he himself provided work on the glebe for those temporarily unemployed so that they would not get into the habit of expecting money without working for it. This, a man of resourcefulness like Duncan could achieve in a parish where there were only 1100 souls; a genius like Chalmers – and there could be few like him – could for a time keep a large industrial parish abreast of its obligations to its less fortunate citizens, but the state take-over was both inevitable and desirable. The parish minister might thereby have lost a certain hold over his parishioners, but an influence that depends on a cash flow in time of need is not a healthy influence. The minister certainly gained by being freed from the difficult duty of interviewing applicants for relief, all the time knowing that the funds at his disposal were too meagre for the circumstances.

If it is somewhat incongruous to think of ministers dabbling in matters of high finance, it is much easier to understand that they were behind many of the attempts to introduce libraries to Scotland's rural communities. The minister's love of books is eternal, and it was very natural that, with the great upsurge in literacy among the working classes of Scotland, the impetus to put good books within their reach should come from those who already treasured well-stocked libraries in their homes. Here again, Duncan in Ruthwell was well to the fore, giving from his own pocket much of the initial capital and many of the first books for his parish library. Very early in this field also – the first in the Secession Church – was John Brown, later of Rose Street, Edinburgh, who started a library in Biggar in 1814; when he left, eight years later, the library contained 143 books. Thomas Guthrie opened one in Arbirlot with the proceeds of a collection taken for this purpose at the opening of his new church: the collection raised £15, which was good when the people's normal Sunday collection, for the poor, was a halfpenny, with the more generous rising to one penny. Guthrie himself comments, 'The £15 left the good people in a state of prostration, exhausted and astonished at their own liberality.' So this commendable scheme spread through the land as minister after minister strove to meet the challenge of parishioners able and eager to read: Balmer in Berwick Secession Church, Charteris in St. Quivox, Ayrshire, and Eadie in Cambridge

Street U.P. were three whose libraries proved very popular, with Eadie's, for example, catering for as many as four hundred readers in a year. Perhaps the most enterprising scheme, however, was devised by Donald Macleod in Lauderdale; establishing a series of mid-week study meetings in various farmhouses throughout the parish, he carried with him each week a knapsack with books which formed an early travelling library: both the meetings and the books proved immensely popular.

When we move now to the minister's position relative to the various public bodies and committees that he would find within his parish area, there are three directions in which we might travel. First of all there would be those ministers who had themselves specialised interests and who would therefore make a point of becoming actively involved in the relevant local body: in this way, for instance, we find that Robertson Nicoll, inducted to Kelso in 1877, served on the committee formed to organise a town band. Of greater assistance to us, however, in establishing an overall picture of the average parish minister and his work, is the second area of community involvement which was open to the occupant of the manse, namely those situations where tradition decreed that a minister should be 'on the committee', and where the ministers normally complied even when the matters discussed were outwith both their interests and their abilities to give knowledgeable advice, and where the expenditure of time could be ill-afforded. Thomas Chalmers explained the dilemma well: 'The peculiarity which bears hardest upon me is the incessant demand on all occasions for the personal attendance of the ministers. They must have four to every funeral or they do not think it has been genteelly gone through. They must have one or more to all the committees of all the societies; they must fall in at every procession; they must attend examinations innumerable, and eat of the dinners consequent upon these examinations; they have a niche assigned them in almost every public doing and that niche must be filled up by them.' As a typical example, Chalmers remarks that, as an ex-officio member of one local committee, he spent an hour in grave deliberation over the future of a gutter.

Over forty years later, the situation was apparently much the same, at least as far as the minister of the Tron Church in Glasgow, Dr. MacGregor, was concerned, for he observes, somewhat testily, 'There is the same insistence on the attendance of the clergy at every committee and at social and philanthropic functions called into being for the waste of time of ministers and laity.' Undoubtedly we can sympathise with the frustrations felt by clergymen whose already full lives were further burdened with what must have seemed trivialities. At the same time, here surely is further eloquent proof that, particularly in the first sixty or seventy years of the nineteenth century, the Church, through its ordained leaders, was consistently given a place in the forefront of society, and he was a wise parish minister who was willing to be seen and heard in the secular side of his community's life.

Thirdly, and probably most important of all, are those public bodies on which the ministers actively sought to serve, in many cases becoming their chairmen and leading organisers. Here it can be difficult to confine oneself narrowly to a strict parish setting; often movements which began within a parish had repercussions over a much wider area. The activities of Stevenson MacGill, licensed in 1790, illustrate this vividly. He was personally involved in establishing a house of refuge for juvenile delinquents, in opening the Magdalene Asylum for females of ill-habits, and in forming a society to help old men in destitution. In addition, in a time of dearth, he actively superintended soup kitchens in the east end of Glasgow. Being concerned for the welfare of prisoners, he published a pamphlet in 1809 on this subject and had the immense satisfaction of seeing many of his suggestions incorporated into the new prison in Paisley.

One whose work owed much to MacGill's example was his biographer, Robert Burns of Paisley. Going to that town in 1811, and remaining there until his emigration to Canada in 1845, Burns was both the faithful parish minister to a very demanding parish, and the devoted pastor to a large congregation. Yet, as Provost Murray rightly says, 'this was only half and probably the lesser half of his labours. In the truest and best sense of the word, he was a citizen of the town; he threw himself with the whole force of his character into every good work; during his long residence, there was no public question, no movement or organisation having for its object the social and political amelioration of the people, or the material, moral, or spiritual wellbeing of the community which did not command

and receive his eloquent advocacy and indefatigable working.' He was connected with Hutchesons' Charity School, was chairman of the directors of the Infirmary, and president for many years of the Philosophical Society. He 'laid great stress on pure water and savings banks' and did much to help poor folk emigrate to New Zealand, Canada and Australia. It would indeed be difficult to conceive of a parish minister with a greater sense of community responsibility, and, as with MacGill, Burns's ideas became famous far beyond his own town; he was the author of the work which, known simply as *Burns on the Poor Law*, was for many years regarded as the standard text book on this and kindred subjects.

While the average parish minister of the nineteenth century was quite prepared to be involved in local social and philanthropic organisations, there were those who felt so keenly the sacred nature of their calling that they could not permit themselves to be caught up in any secular deliberations, however praiseworthy. A. J. Campbell speaks of those Evangelicals who had a mind 'ever suspicious of any activity which was not professedly religious', and examples in support are not lacking. The *Evangelical Magazine* in 1810 quotes this extract from the diary of a deceased minister: 'Let me never sit long with any of my people who do not talk about their souls; I find the company of carnal persons, though they may not be very immoral, injurious to my soul.' Andrew Bonar records in his diary that on occasion he felt unsettled because he had been 'conversing much with men and was much outwardly engaged'; elsewhere he says that he counted it as a 'leisure not often indulged in to have a few hours without much thought of God'. Such men could not have countenanced discussing Chalmers's gutter for even five minutes, but they were, thankfully, in the decided minority, and their numbers grew steadily less as the century progressed.

As a postscript, there are two matters to which we must refer briefly. First there are the great efforts on the part of James Begg, Free Church minister in Newington, Edinburgh, to improve the lot of the working classes generally. We have admired already his nation-wide agitation to improve housing standards. He was also largely responsible for securing the Saturday half-holiday for shopkeepers; he campaigned successfully to have Princes Street Gardens opened free to the public, and he was to the fore in attempts to have adequate wash houses and model lodging houses established in Edinburgh. His ecclesiastical opponents might christen him 'the evil genius of the Free Church' because of his opposition to the proposed union between the Free Church and the United Presbyterian Church in the 1860s and 1870s, but he remains a devoted parish minister of real vision whose ideas, like those of MacGill and Burns before him, reached out in triumph to cover the nation.

Secondly, we glance at the nineteenth-century parish minister's opportunities for influencing the political opinions of his people. In general terms, it was held to be unwise for a minister to declare too emphatically his party allegiance lest he should seem to clothe his personal opinions on these secular matters with the authority belonging to his sacred office. In this way, Patrick Brewster, inducted as minister of the second charge of Paisley Abbey in 1818, found himself in considerable ecclesiastical hot water over his championing of the Chartist cause, while no less commanding a personality than Dr. Alexander Whyte of St. George's, Edinburgh, received a letter from thirteen of his prominent members, including eight elders, expressing the opinion that 'a minister cannot give active support to a political party in matters of acute public controversy without to a greater or lesser extent compromising his congregation'. This letter was reaction to Whyte's publicly declared views on the vexed Irish question, and thereafter, although he cherished his political convictions every bit as ardently as before, 'he scrupulously refrained from giving any public sign of his political faith'. Brewster's troubles, on the other hand, stretched over eight years and involved him in protracted hearings before Presbyteries and Commissions of the General Assembly. In addition, the Commanding Officer of one of the regiments stationed in Paisley issued an order prohibiting his men from attending the Abbey Church on the days when Brewster preached because of certain insulting references to the military. All the Chartists' main aims, save the extreme plea for annual Parliaments, have long since been granted, and we would not today consider anyone, Christian minister or not, dangerously extreme in advocating policies which included manhood suffrage, vote by ballot, equal electoral districts, and payment for members of Parliament. Brewster's 'crime' was that, while a parish minister, he had become actively involved in political matters and had asserted his particular views on controversial issues with no little vehemence.

In the main the ministers accepted the need to be politically impartial in public pronouncements, although they reserved the right to speak out boldly on matters which, though they belonged ultimately in the realm of the professional politicians, involved definite Christian principles. Three examples will explain: Andrew Thomson and many of his colleagues worked actively to end the slave trade in the colonies; Burns and others saw a Christian interest in the repeal of the Corn Laws and the introduction of Free Trade; 1600 ministers, including almost all the ministers of the Free and U.P. Churches, signed a petition which was sent to Gladstone regarding the defence of the Christians in the Turkish Empire against the Russians. On such issues, ministers mounted public platforms and rushed into print in strong-worded pamphlets, and their people, realising the Christian concern that motivated their actions, did not register any widespread protest.

It was, however, true in the nineteenth century, as it will be true in any age, that the well-loved and respected minister was able to influence many of his people politically, and this without any conscious or deliberate effort. A sentence from the biography of Robert Burns is apt: 'He declined to descend to the political arena but did not deem it inconsistent with the sacredness of his office or as calculated to rub off his clerical enamel to indicate distinctly his political preferences.' Many of his colleagues declined to be so specific, but in parish after parish, the flock who devotedly followed their pastor's leading in things spiritual, were frequently influenced by him in matters political even although no word of party controversy ever passed his lips in public.

Chapter 8

I pray not that thou shouldest take them out of the world

In contrast to the minister's official and public roles, we turn now to his more personal and domestic pursuits often as head of a large manse family. Particularly in the early years of the century, the minister's family was often to be pitied. Many of the stipends were none too generous; the manse, as we shall see in more detail in a later chapter, was expected to provide hospitality to all comers, with the result that the manse wife had often to show great ingenuity in keeping her own family adequately fed and clothed. To bolster the domestic economy, therefore, she frequently acquired skills in spinning and in making blankets, while other regular manse industries were tanning, salting, and the making of butter, cheese, and candles. As a matter of course, the minister's wife and children assisted actively in the farm work of the glebe and in looking after the sheep and cattle which provided them with additional sources of revenue.

The manse children's lot in life was made more difficult still by the very fact of which we have become increasingly aware, namely that their father's life was so crowded that he was prevented from spending much time with them. Thomas Guthrie, for example, speaks of the 'sad fate' of many Edinburgh manse families where the ministers, 'spending the whole day in the service of the public, retire to spend the evenings within their studies away from the children, whose ill habits and ill doing in their future career showed how far they had been sacrificed on the altar of public duty'. Extreme though this may be, it does highlight an all too common failing in manse life where young children, assured by their mothers that they had a spiritual Father, were too dependent on the same source for information on their earthly father. For his part, Guthrie wisely resolved to spend as many evenings as possible in the parlour with his children, while Candlish and Rainy were two more who, though unceasingly busy on official matters, always sought to make time for entering into their children's games and interests. How effectively even busy men could do this is seen in Candlish's biography. When his children were anticipating and planning some amusement, and found that at that time their father was to be from home, they gladly postponed the time of their expected enjoyment for the sake of his companionship in it. 'We will wait,' they said, 'till he comes back that we may have some fun.' With too many, however, the effort was not made, and the children grew up remote from their fathers; inevitably, as the century progressed and as the ministers' commitments by way of week-night activities increased, this threat to manse family life increased.

If outside duties were thus allowed to deny the minister a well-balanced family life, only rarely was even the busiest cleric willing to forgo his daily hours of private study, reading and meditation. To this end, many a manse study was occupied from a very early hour each morning as, in quietness and solitude, the occupant devoted himself to his books and his prayers. No matter how late it had been when the previous night's rest had begun, and regardless of how hectic a day stretched out before him, the average minister felt as did Robert Murray McCheyne, that 'prayer is the initial necessity of every day': 'I feel it is far better to begin with God', he said, 'to see His face first, and to get my soul near Him before it is near another.' Duncan in Ruthwell frequently rose as early as 4 a.m.: Thomas Guthrie, and Thomas Gardiner, minister of Old Machar Free Church, Aberdeen, from 1861, were regularly at work by 5 a.m., and Norman Macleod, Murray McCheyne, Andrew Bonar, and Archibald Charteris were just four of many who never lay in bed beyond 6 a.m. In very few instances can we even suspect that this practice was followed for any other reason than from the desire to have these uninterrupted hours of prayer and study before facing the non-stop business of the day. It is, however, possible to echo the sentiments of the Rev. John Watson, minister in Liverpool from 1880, who, noting the early morning habits of his clerical forefathers and realising his own fondness for lying long of a winter morning, commented, 'This early rising was a needless irritation unto the generation following.' But credit must be given for these men's determination to study and to pray at the one hour of the day when they were unlikely to be interrupted. There is just occasionally a suggestion that the early risers may have imagined that self-punishment in the name of religion was pleasing to God, as, for instance, in the case of Alexander Moody Stuart, minister of Free St. Luke's, Edinburgh, following the Disruption. Each night, during the night, he awoke every hour and a half or two hours, struck a light, and stood to read a few verses of the Bible.

In the vast majority of cases the study lights that burned regularly from 6 a.m. until 9 a.m. did so for the best reasons, and in that period each day whole chapters of the Scriptures were lovingly committed to memory, the latest devotional literature and Biblical commentaries were combed and summarised in personal note books, and detailed personalised prayers were offered both for the world and for the local parish. Indeed, in many parishes, these hours of study were continued after a brief interruption for breakfast. Donald John Martin in Stornoway and Alexander Somerville in Anderston regularly went to their Churches during this period of the morning and prayed for their congregations by name in each pew. It is impossible to assess the effects for good that such a careful and disciplined life of study and devotion must have had on both pastor and flock. The minister's mind would be continually filled and re-filled with thoughts and ideas that would help both in his pastoral work and in his sermon preparation. So far as the congregations were concerned, if we believe at all in the power of prayer, we must believe that these hours paved the way for many great works of the Holy Spirit.

Nineteenth-century ministers had two conflicting attitudes towards their hobbies and leisure activities. There were those like Andrew Bonar and Murray McCheyne who did not consider it right for a minister to have 'free' time to squander on secular pleasures, however harmless these pleasures might in themselves be. There were clerics who enjoyed their moments of relaxation and indulged in the innocent sports of the laymen. Donald John Martin, Archibald Scott, and Principal Story, for example, had a great passion for golf and played the game with enthusiasm and no little skill. In addition, and rather predictably out on a limb, Alexander Carlyle favoured theatre-going and card playing at a time when both occupations were firmly closed to ministers, and he made a public show of participating in dancing and billiards which were only slightly less unorthodox pursuits for one of his sacred calling. As in other aspects of his ministry, however, he was, both in the nature of his hobbies and in the time he spent on them, an individualist. It is interesting to realise that though theatre-going was slow to gain official approval as a pleasure fit for the clergy, it nevertheless gained steadily, if stealthily, in ministerial popularity. As early as 1784, important business at the General Assembly had to be arranged only for those days when the celebrated actress, Mrs. Siddons, was not appearing in the Edinburgh playhouse, for when she was billed to be on stage, 'all the younger members of the Assembly, clergy as well as laity, took their stations in the theatre by three in the afternoon'. The story is told of how Dr. James MacGregor, minister of Glasgow's Tron Church, was spotted by an elder in London's Adelphi Theatre in 1866. The douce elder naturally threatened to report this grave breach of decorum to the congregation, to which MacGregor replied, 'They won't believe you, so you need not tell them.'

Among those ministers who disapproved thoroughly of men of the cloth finding moments of God-given time to fritter away in secular trivialities, Andrew Bonar counted it 'a leisure not often indulged in to have a few hours without much thought of God'; in fact, his diaries make it abundantly plain that he ultimately came to regard such hours as more of a definite sin than as a permitted break from duty. Murray McCheyne was similarly unbending. There were few things he dreaded more than 'worldly amusements' in the families of professing Christians, especially ministers: 'The extent to which novel reading, dancing parties, private theatricals, card playing, luxurious feasting and dressing, loose, frivolous and profane song singing, with other exhibitions of utter worldliness, prevail even in professedly Christian families with the sanction and under the eye of office-bearers of the Church would hardly be believed.' To any catalogue of ministerial pastimes, such men's lives could contribute nothing, for not even on Saturday or Sunday evenings could such as Bonar unbend; rather did he interpret it as the direct work of Satan himself when thoughts entered his head that might turn his attention momentarily to things other than the direct work of the ministry.

As we would expect, it was within the Free Church, and particularly in the Highland areas, that such rigid views were most pronounced. Dancing was a favourite object of attack: for example, the Rev. A. M. Bannatyne, minister of Union Free Church, Aberdeen, from 1886 to 1890, delivered a stinging attack in Presbytery on what he christened 'flings and springs and close-bosomed whirlings'. Professor Ian Henderson is surely correct when he states that this section of Free Church opinion 'fell into line with the straiter English sects and began to damn harmless amusements'.

The majority of Scotland's ministers, however, realised the benefits to body and mind of a few hours' recreation, with the result that angling, hunting, rambling, cricket, croquet, chess, botany, and novel reading all had their clerical patrons. Prime favourite, then as now, was undoubtedly golf even in those areas where the more narrow-minded in the congregations felt that a lusty swinging of wooden clubs was hardly a fit occupation for a man of God. In Stornoway, for example, Donald John Martin – a Free Church minister incidentally – was something of a golfing fanatic, a fact which scandalised his parishioners. They felt that their minister should scorn all forms of secular amusement and be dressed at all times in broadcloth and silk hat. When, therefore, Martin persisted in his outrageous indulgence, his clubs were openly branded as 'the clubs of Satan' and not a few folk walked out of a neighbouring church when he appeared there as an assistant at the Communion Season.

Otherwise, the people of Scotland were reasonably content that their ministers should manage time off for seemly recreation. For the very busy – Norman Macleod and Alexander Whyte, for instance – this amounted often to nothing more than a few hours' leisurely walking on a Saturday afternoon, or a few hours somewhere in the week during which a favourite periodical could be read, but the principle was good and generally accepted. We would agree with the view of A. K. H. Boyd who felt that ministerial participation in popular sports could help regulate the conduct of such sports and could lead to a closer link between the Church and the ordinary people: 'I have known injudicious clergymen,' writes Boyd, 'who did all they could to discourage the games and sports of their parishioners. They could not prevent them, but one thing they did, they made them disreputable. They made sure that the poor man who ran in a sack or climbed a greased pole felt that thereby he was forfeiting his character, perhaps imperilling his salvation.'

It might scarcely be correct to include in the list of ministerial hobbies the willingness to farm the glebe. With too many it was a matter of absolute necessity that their glebes should be made to yield the maximum income to augment the official stipend. At the same time, farming in this way was honestly enjoyed by many of the ministers: it provided healthy exercise, and it afforded a non-ecclesiastical occupation which was universally approved for men of the cloth. Elders who might frown at the sight of their minister wielding a golf club gave fullest blessing to the same man deploying a spade in the tilling of God's own earth. With some ministers, however, glebe-farming developed until it became neither a mere hobby nor a straightforward economic operation; in not a few instances, these farms became the model farms in their areas, with many sound agricultural improvements being introduced in the minister's fields. Henry Duncan in Ruthwell had a large glebe of some fifty acres and it was among the most advanced in the country so far as farming methods were concerned. 'Though originally a sterile soil, Duncan's glebe had become the most productive farmland in the neighbourhood; he felt it a duty to show an example here; many were the experiments in draining, in ploughing, in reaping etc., which, from time to time, were made under his inspection.' All this was commendable enough in the cause of good agriculture, but it had the added benefit in that Duncan's parishioners were able to benefit directly from his determination to keep making improvements to his glebe. When other employment in the area was scarce, he was able to give them work in ditching, draining, and generally improving the manse grounds. In Ellon, too, there was a very fine glebe farm run by the parish minister, the future Professor Robertson. He was a pioneer in many successful experiments in farming procedure and he was the first in Britain to introduce a new method of manuring which proved both popular and successful. Of the many other names we could cite when speaking of notable ministerial farmers, that of Dr. John Gillespie deserves special mention. Minister of Mousewald near Dumfries and a Moderator of the Church, he had such an active and expert interest in farming that he was known as 'the minister of agriculture for Scotland'.

If farming could only marginally be termed a ministerial hobby, then equally reading and the accumulation of books might be thought of as part and parcel of every minister's working life and not as a special feature of leisure hours. Nevertheless, it is remarkable to see the extent to which, with many men, this became almost an obsession. Quite apart from their hours of study each morning for which the purchase of theological books was essential, and outwith the efforts of many to establish parish libraries, many a minister built up personal libraries which, in sheer size and in the wealth of topics fully covered, are truly remarkable. Robertson Nicoll's father was minister of Lumsden Free Church. His income never reached £200 a year, yet he built up a library of 17,000 books. 'Every shilling he could spare from a strictly frugal life went to the enlargement of his library.' 'In later years he began to buy duplicates, for as he said to his son, "You are never really safe with one copy of a good book." ' If Nicoll went to extreme lengths to satisfy his bibliomania, the spirit that motivated him was at work in many a manse: likewise, the more learned journals found a home with great ease in the manse drawing-rooms. *The Spectator*, *The New Statesman*, and *The Saturday Review* were three staunch favourites: indeed we are told that 'the first habit which Alexander Whyte taught his young wife was to read *The Spectator* regularly'. The one area of non-professional reading which was somewhat suspect for many a day was the reading of novels. Quite apart from the predictable disapproval of the Bonars and the McCheynes, there were many who could not comfortably commend unlimited reading of this type of fiction. Dr. James MacGregor of St. Cuthbert's, Edinburgh, greatly enjoyed a novel but all along his motto was that a little at a time was quite sufficient: 'A good novel now and then is a good thing; but novel reading as a regular rule and practice is about as dangerous a thing as I know.' The fear was that, as well as being untrue, their stories might be unreal and develop in the mind the taste for reading without thinking or without relating what was read to the hard practicalities of life and work. Dr. Marcus

Dods appears to have reached a convenient compromise: rebuked gently by his colleagues for reading so many of the 'lighter' books, he demonstrated time and again that 'he did not turn over the leaves of the most ephemeral publication without taking something out of it for his pulpit and platform lectures'.

Underlying all this, however, there is a much more basic question. Whether a minister should have played golf or read popular novels during the nineteenth century is interesting enough; more important is the extent to which the ministers felt that they should be fully part of this world. Particularly within the Free Church there did seem to be a belief that this world mattered very little; we remarked earlier that certain preachers and evangelists had little or no social message – the salvation of men's souls was all that mattered to them – and that meant that the next world had to be so meticulously prepared for that there was little time for bothering about conditions in this life. There were several notable ministers who lived out their whole lives in a somewhat rarefied atmosphere where every thought, word, and deed had to be entirely religious in content, and we might respectfully wonder whether this could ever be the correct attitude of mind for one whose calling was to proclaim the Good News of Christ.

In a way, this is the continuation of the old extreme Moderate versus extreme Evangelical controversy, but there was more to it when this conflict of attitudes persisted, and in some ways even grew as the nineteenth century advanced. Andrew Bonar felt that every moment of every day had to be spent in direct awareness of God; even walking from one house call to another he would 'redeem the time' by praying. He was genuinely worried one holiday season when he saw his family 'so full of spirits in the country that they may have for the time bidden farewell to God in their heart'. In some ways, Bonar is extreme, but in many other ways he symbolises the attitude of mind of certain of his influential Free Church brethren. They could never, even for a moment, 'put off the clergyman' no matter what they were doing. John Milne, for example, would never have been mistaken for anything but the Free Church minister that he was. Horatius Bonar says of him, 'I may safely say that he never wrote a letter, however short, without some sentence or word or leaflet that spoke the man of God. . . . If he met a man in the street, he had some ready word of peace to greet him with. If he went into a shop, he would take occasion from the articles he was buying to say a word in season. If he drove in a cab, he would not part from the cabman till he had given him some little book or spoken some text or reminded him of his higher calling. . . . He did not feel he had done anything undignified when, one evening in the streets of Perth, he gave full chase to three boys who ran away from him as he was trying to persuade them to come to his Sabbath School; nor did he think he had done anything out of the way when he got up on the engine, amid smoke and dust, and drove along for a stage in order to talk with the driver and the stoker.' Of the same mind was James Robertson of Newington U.P. Church: 'When he was travelling by railway, or walking in a country road, or entering a house on a casual errand, he was looking out for opportunities for dropping a seed word'; for example, when arriving home in a cab, the door was never opened for him at once as it was known he would always talk ten minutes with the cabman as part of his 'wayside sowing'.

With such men – and we could detail similar behaviour on the part of W. C. Burns, Murray McCheyne, and others – talk of hobbies or no hobbies is only scraping the surface. The question is whether the aim of being 100 per cent clergymen all the time should ever be the ideal, whatever the century, or in fact whether such uncompromising piety can discourage honest men and women from attempting to live Christian lives within the framework of the organised Church. In addition, there must be a suspicion that human life, as God meant it to be, is distorted if two watertight compartments, the sacred and the secular, are artificially created. In the present day, it is comparatively easy, particularly in the towns and cities, for worshippers to move their allegiance from one congregation to another if they feel out of sympathy with a minister's view of what the Christian faith entails. In the nineteenth century things were rather less easy; it was difficult for a person to 'turn' from the Free Church to the Established Church because personal bitterness between the two continued for many years. It did happen, therefore, that some devout folk, uncomfortable under the ministries of narrow Free Kirkers, were to all intents and purposes lost to the Christian Church. Admittedly, the Church never did exist to win support by preaching only what the people wanted to hear, but it must be questioned whether the Bonars and Milnes really preached the whole truth. As the century progressed, as travel and education broadened the Scotsman's mind, as the Church had to face greater competition for men's time and interest, a too narrow approach to living could only make the more human parishioners feel that perhaps Christianity was not for them.

Humour is for most men an invaluable and God-given part of their personality. Again, however, humour found little or no place in the lives of the Bonars and Milnes, and this contrasts greatly with other notable ministers in both the Free and the Established Churches. Thomas Guthrie and Archibald Scott, for example, had a great creative ability in humour, although, quite rightly in view of the times in which they lived, it did not intrude in the pulpit: 'I never saw a shadow of a smile pass over the congregation of Free St. John's', says Dr. Hanna, a colleague of Guthrie's. In private conversations, however, it was a very different matter, and their flashes of genuine wit, though never boisterous or undignified, won many friends. Norman Macleod, too, was gifted in this way, being a particularly able cartoonist and mimic. In his student days, some of his family feared that he might be too full of fun to be a fit and acceptable minister of the Gospel. Their fears were groundless, however, as he always kept his infectious humour in its proper place. Donald John Martin – in many ways as serious and devout a man as one could wish to meet – was another whose great, almost uncontrollable, sense of fun outside of the pulpit greatly enhanced his appeal.

There is today a fear that the world may be exercising a pull to lead men away from the Church; without being too hard on thoroughly sincere men, it may seem that in the last century there were those clergymen who were trying hard to pull the Church totally away from the world. In short, our opinion would be that Professor W. Garden Blaikie offered wise advice to the students of New College when he said, 'Gravity or seriousness should lie at the foundation of the character of the Christian minister, but a little playfulness of character in private has a wonderful opening effect, especially on the young.'

Chapter 9

I was an hungered, and ye gave me meat: I was a stranger, and ye took me in

The manse occupied a special place in the eyes of most Scotsmen. The minister's house was not just his private place of residence but was the haven and sanctuary to which all in any kind of need could confidently go. Even in the days when many of the ministers presented a rather severe front to the lower mortals around them, the Scottish manse was fairly universally regarded as the natural 'port' to make for in any storm. As more clergymen came to exhibit a genuine and friendly interest in their people's domestic affairs, this custom waxed stronger, with those who went out of their way to care for the poorer classes reaping a vast harvest of house callers. It was said of Robert Burns of Paisley, for example, that 'long rows of poverty-stricken people reached out from his study desk into the street, eager to pour into his ready ear the diary of their woes'. Thomas Guthrie said that each day his Edinburgh home was 'besieged by crowds of half-naked creatures, men, women and children shivering with cold and hunger'. Norman Macleod of the Barony felt that the Devil should be renamed BELLzebub because of the many interruptions suffered by hard-working ministers who were trying to snatch a few hours undisturbed in the seclusion of their studies. Dr. James MacGregor of St. Cuthbert's, Edinburgh, felt this burden equally heavy; when in Paisley (1855–1862), he said that these interruptions were the 'hardest cross' of his profession.

Those in need in the nineteenth century had few avenues of help open to them. Until 1845, the minister and kirk session controlled parish poor relief; with educational standards low, it was natural in official business to turn to the minister for guidance, and indeed it is revealing to see the faith which helpless men and women had in their ministers. It is to the lasting credit of our clerical forefathers that, generally speaking, this faith was not misplaced. In truth, the minister had to be ready to deal with any kind of problem, and each ring at the doorbell threatened something quite new. Norman Macleod's grandfather in Morven often found that he had to be both lawyer and judge in settling a feud between individuals or even between whole families. The elder Story in Rosneath was frequently interrupted in the midst of his studies by parties who felt that he should be free without notice to show them personally over the near-by glen. Mr. Bower, minister of Old Monkland early in the nineteenth century, opened his door on more than one occasion to find a disgruntled woman parishioner bearing her breakfast plate of porridge which he was asked to examine as evidence that her husband did not provide her with sufficient to eat.

In the main, however, the callers at the manse were seeking assistance with employment, clothing, food or money. Not all ministers were in a position to do what we saw Henry Duncan could do in Ruthwell and personally employ such people on the glebe, but many could, by their position of influence, find work for the willing person. John Macleod in Govan, for instance, was particularly noted for this, and his was the first name mentioned in his parish by those who found themselves out of work – 'they had unbounded faith in the Doctor's omnipotent ability to get them work', and he frequently succeeded. To meet the incessant demand for warm clothing for the winter, some churches formed clothing societies where a central reserve of good usable clothes was kept. Thomas Guthrie and Norman Macleod were two ministers who organised such a society to great effect. In practice, however, it was generally left to the minister and his wife to cope with this problem with the result that many manses became almost second-hand clothes markets. It took great ingenuity to keep supply ahead of the very firm demand and in those instances where supplies did fail, it was not uncommon for the minister to give of his own private wardrobe. A. D. Grant of Mount Park Free Church, Greenock, was forever appearing in a new coat while some needy person would be noticed wearing his previous one. Donald John Martin's generosity went even further on one occasion; he gave away his last pair of trousers and had to spend the rest of the day in bed while his tailor hurriedly produced replacements.

The unselfish willingness of the clergy to meet the needs of those who poured out doorstep tales of hardship is seen most clearly in the amount of hard cash which changed hands in these circumstances. Not only did well-known and trusted parishioners receive hand-outs in this way, but the itinerant poor, who might never have been in the parish before and who might never again return to it, had their purses lined also. G. H. C. Macgregor, both in the East Free Church, Aberdeen, and in his later London charge in Notting Hill, adopted a strict practice of tithing all his income from all sources, with one tenth being set aside to meet personal appeals for help. William Robertson, minister of Irvine U.P. Church from 1843, was similarly systematic but further increased his generosity to good causes by consistently doubling the largest subscription given by any other individual to appeals of which he approved. Stevenson MacGill, minister of Glasgow's Tron Church at the beginning of the nineteenth century, was open-handed to the point of recklessness in that he got himself into debt on a number of occasions because of the large sums he gave away, while in Perth, John Milne made it his practice to go to the bank each month, pay outstanding bills, and there and then give the balance in his account to the poor. No praise can be too high for such acts of Christian charity which, with many, became almost an obsession, so determined were they that they should do all in their power to help their less fortunate brothers. Indeed, we could point to those whose zeal in this direction bordered on eccentricity. J. P. Struthers in Greenock, for example, made a point of diluting his ink with water, thereby saving around threepence a year; this money, with the proceeds of other economies, went to charitable purposes.

Callers at the manse door could go away with high hopes of a job; they might well have silver in new-found pockets, and as often as not they would enjoy a warming bowl of soup in the kitchen before moving on. In the north of Scotland, however, and particularly in the early years of the last century, manse hospitality did not end there. On occasion, the callers might express a wish to remain within the manse for a period of days or weeks until their fortunes might improve, and, incredible though it must sound to our rather more inhospitable ears, many manse families did keep 'open house' in this way and provide what amounted to free hotels. In the parish of Morven, Norman Macleod's grandfather had a family of sixteen; in addition, he had, living in cottages on the glebe, various shepherds, boatmen, and ploughmen, who were, to some degree, maintained by him. For all that, he still managed to stretch his house and his stipend to care for the tourists, the traders, and the 'gentlemen of the road' who automatically gravitated to the manse. In Ruthwell, Dr. Duncan similarly threw open his own door to many friendless folk who stayed more or less as long as they pleased. In Rosneath, the elder Story's roll of visitors could total a dozen or more in a single day, ranging 'from the peer to the peasant', with the 'old companion, the needy suppliant, the hungry tourist, and the perplexed foreigner' all turning to him for help; nor was any caller ever disappointed, for, as his son remarks, 'the manse door was like the heart of its owner, ever standing open to receive all who chose to enter'; no matter his rank, each visitor 'was received and entertained with the most expansive hospitality and goodwill'.

Principal Rainy's grandfather was minister of Creich at the end of the eighteenth century; the picture of life in that Sutherland manse shows well the situation that held good in many similar manses throughout Scotland as the nineteenth century opened: 'The manse had almost a public function, for there was no inn near and people arrived at all hours to find shelter and a welcome.' It was not a large house but it was run on the principle that 'where there is heart-room, there is house-room. . . . On Saturday evenings and Sundays the manse was always quite full as many came great distances to Church'; it was thought no unfair imposition that they should spend a good part of the week-end at the manse; in addition, as we saw in Morven and Ruthwell, 'the manse was seldom without one or two friends or acquaintances who, being in reduced circumstances, were invited to stay in the manse'. Norman Macleod is surely correct when he sums it up in this way: 'The ingenuity with which guests were accommodated in the manse was equalled only by the skill with which a very limited income was made to cover the expense of house-keeping and looking after a large family. . . . No manse was ever so full but that, like a bus, one more could be taken in.' Perhaps the most penetrating observation, however, comes from one of Thomas Guthrie's servants in Edinburgh who had seen previous service in a small inn: 'This house is just like a public, only there's nae sillar comes in.'

It is not unreasonable, in the light of what has gone before, to ask how well paid the minister of the nineteenth century was. The answer, in all but the really well-to-do parishes, is surprising. For ministers with no private income to supplement their stipend, the sum of money they would normally receive was often on the low side for ordinary recurring needs. Indeed, right from his student days, a minister could find himself in real financial difficulties. Today, a divinity student can eke out his bursaries and grants by undertaking pulpit supply: we have already noted that in the nineteenth century this practice was actively discouraged. In addition, we saw that the student's plight was made worse by the allocation of bursaries according to the patrons' whims and not according to ability or need. Even when licensed, however, a minister's financial worries were not at an end. Until the Disruption of 1843 created an immediate need for some 500 additional ministers in Scotland, supply regularly exceeded demand, with the result that many men, some very distinguished scholars among them, had to wait for several years before entering their first charge. Figures are difficult to come by, but it appears that in the first thirty years of the nineteenth century, an average of 150 students were licensed each year, while the normal number of vacancies occurring in any one year was not much above 30. The Colonies and the Mission Fields attracted some; others resorted to teaching; the remainder lived a Micawber-like existence 'waiting for something to turn up'. Marcus Dods, later to be Principal of New College, had to wait for eight years and be rejected by twenty-one vacant congregations before he received a call. Robert Candlish of St. George's, Edinburgh, languished well over two years, while Cameron Lees and James MacGregor, later to be two of Edinburgh's most distinguished ministers, both began to learn Gaelic in the hope that this might open the door to a church more quickly, even if it were in a remote highland glen. As if the system were not bad enough prior to a man receiving and accepting a call, monetary problems pursued the minister right into his hard-won manse. Rural charges, the normal scene of a first ministry, did not pay large stipends; their large manses demanded more furniture than any probationer could easily buy; and, rubbing salt deep in the wounds, the considerable expenses of the induction were the minister's personal responsibility.

Thomas Guthrie's experiences illustrate perfectly the shortcomings of the whole set-up. He had to while away as profitably as he could five years between licence and ordination; he had been at university preparing for the ministry for a period of ten years, and in those fifteen years – 'five as a journeyman, ten as an apprentice' – he had received only five guineas in the Church's service. Yet, when his induction to Arbirlot finally arrived in 1830, he was presented with a bill for £60 – £30 to cover Crown fees, and a similar sum to finance the dinner he had to provide for members of the Presbytery and the local gentry. When he negotiated this last hurdle and surveyed his new responsibilities, generous, even adequate, financial recompense still seemed a long way off: not in bitterness but rather in honesty did he see his paltry stipend more as a 'starving' than a 'living', commenting that 'some gentlemen pay their French cooks, and many merchants their clerks, a larger salary than he receives who has charge of their souls, and in whom they expect the piety of an apostle, the accomplishments of a scholar, and the manners of a gentleman'. Guthrie was not mercenary; he was in no sense a hireling. The sense of the injustice of the situation, however, was to remain with him right through his ministry even when he personally was receiving a much more adequate stipend in Edinburgh, and in his address as Moderator in 1862 he showed clearly his feelings: 'I would tempt no man to enter the Church by the hope of wealth, but I wish no man to be deterred from it by the certainty of poverty: that stands as a barrier at the moment – I don't say between the Church and the higher classes, but between the Church and the middle classes of society.'

Guthrie's financial plight is cited, partly because his experience gives abundant proof of shortcomings in the whole monetary structure of the Church relative to its ordained servants, and partly because we have already seen enough of that man's great work for Christ to respect his opinions. His views are fully supported by many of his colleagues throughout the nineteenth century. In the early years of the century, for example, Jupiter Carlyle commented that 'the stipends keep no pace with the rising prosperity of the country, and the ministers are degraded in their rank by the increasing wealth of the inferior orders'. In the 1830s, the parish minister of Ellon – the future Professor Robertson – was forced to live away from the manse for the first two years of his ministry because he could not afford to furnish and maintain its vast size. The next decade saw John Caird struggling to cope in Newton-on-Ayr with what Charles Warr labelled a 'starvation stipend', and as late as the mid 1870s, Professor Blaikie felt it no exaggeration to state that 'in the great majority of cases the minister is subject to considerable financial pressure and needs a self-denial that amounts to heroism'. Without doubt, however, the most disturbing allegation is made by Andrew Somerville, Secession minister in Dumbarton from 1830 to 1845: in his autobiography he claims that 'it is an ascertained fact that more ministers die in the first three years of their ministry than in the next ten years', adding that this was so because financial hardship and resultant poor feeding in student days undermined their health to such a degree that they could not stand the strain of leading a congregation. In evidence he too quotes the case of Thomas Guthrie who, though the son of the Provost of Brechin, could afford to eat meat only twice in a six-month college session; with him, as with the vast majority of students of his day, oatmeal was the standard daily diet.

If we accept these statements at their face value, a fascinating side-issue raises itself. In nineteenth-century Scotland, it was fairly generally the case that ministers' wives were drawn from the upper levels of society. The lairds, the landed gentry, and the titled families considered it amply fitting that their daughters should marry into the Church. If congregations benefited from having their 'first ladies' thus able to take a lead in social and educational work within the parish, many a minister found in this tradition, and in the handsome dowry and regular private income that often accompanied it, nothing less than the means of financial salvation, a fact that was not lost on the clergy as a whole. The *Evangelical Magazine* in 1822 carried an article openly alleging that, because of inadequate stipends, there were ministers who made money 'the principal object of pursuit' in women to be their wives. In Rosneath, the elder Story, who had just seen a lady reject his proposal of marriage, was given this pointed advice by a friend: 'If you marry a wife without money, you are ruined for life; it is all stuff about a "treasure in herself"; you are not a money-making man but you are sufficiently inclined to be an expensive one and therefore you must get money with your wife.' Not all ministers who married well did so purely for financial convenience, but, even subconsciously, the thought would be there and may well have helped cement into marriage many a blossoming friendship.

On the same domestic front, many ministers regarded it as inherently desirable that they should have a wife right through their active parish ministry. That is, if a first or second wife was snatched away in childbirth or by some outbreak of fever (two events that occurred with distressing frequency) the minister often consciously sought a successor after a seemly time – generally regarded as a year – had been allowed to elapse. The overriding reason for this was domestic rather than parochial or emotional. It was not often that the widower cleric craved prompt remarriage from the thought of what a wife could achieve within the church or parish; rather he was fearful of mounting confusion in the ordering of the affairs of his own house, and when the implications of this fact sink home we may feel it necessary to revise our views on the poverty of the average minister. Throughout almost all of the last century, even the poorest manses had their servants. The minister had to be away from home a good deal on official business and so could not, from this reason alone, adequately supervise these servants; a suitable wife, coming in all probability from a household in which several servants had been employed, was an invaluable 'foreman' in the manse kitchen to ensure that the various home industries were kept on profitable lines. This last fact, undeniable though it is, must make us ask a definition of the poverty that our clerical forefathers were said to suffer. Today a manse servant is something of a rarity; the minimum stipend does not, unaided, stretch to such assistance, and yet 'poverty' would hardly describe the condition of modern servant-less manses. For the nineteenth-century minister, however, it was quite unthinkable to be without at least two servants; his position in the community demanded it. W. G. Blaikie, inducted to the very modest parish of Drumblade in 1842, employed a man for the glebe, a maid for the house, and a girl for the cows and poultry. By the same token, when A. K. H. Boyd of St. Andrews wished to describe a manse where there was poverty, he began, as we today might, by pointing to bare carpets, unkept gardens, and a library too devoid of books; his last example, however, is drawn straight from the thinking of the last century – 'the servants are of the inferior class, coarse and insolent'.

A minister's poverty was relative only to the special position he occupied in society. He could not live as his ordinary parishioners lived; he had to maintain his manse so that it was on a par with the stately residences of the local gentry; his high-born wife must not be asked to undertake menial tasks which she had not known in her father's house. Therefore, while his stipend might well have supported him in discreet comfort, it had to be strained to the limits to elevate himself and his family to the socially approved level. To this extent, the minister was something of a prisoner to middle and upper class tradition and convention even within the four walls of his own house. Generally speaking, Scotland drew her ministers from the middle classes and not from the aristocracy, with the result that they needed the approval of the wealthy benefactors who would not take kindly to one who too easily fraternised with the inferior social orders. It was a cruel dilemma for many an honest man who realised full well that the charge that the ministry were remote from the poorer people had a measure of truth which would not easily be countered or eliminated.

In short, it was difficult for an ordinary minister effectively to rebel against tradition in this matter, a fact which is surely emphasised by the many examples of parish ministers being given very large gifts by their congregations to mark some milestone in their lives. Even though stipends might be generally low, such presentations could soar to extreme generosity; obviously, it was the wealthier classes who could contribute most meaningfully to such gifts and therefore it was at all times expedient for a minister not to appear out of sympathy with his potential benefactors' way of life. Silver plate, silver candlesticks, and gold watches were the most popular of the routine gifts; on retiral, or on attaining one's jubilee, however, the amount of hard cash forthcoming could be quite startling. When Dr. Cunningham retired, he received no less than £6900; Dr. Candlish was given £5600, while Dr. Guthrie and Principal

Rainy both collected £5000. When Andrew Bonar celebrated fifty years in the ministry, his Finnieston congregation presented him with £4000, and in Liverpool, Dr. Watson (Ian Maclaren) received a cheque for £2600 to make his hours of pensioner ease as enjoyable as possible. Admittedly, these figures refer to noted public personalities to whose testimonials many outwith mere parish surroundings would gladly contribute, but even in the ordinary parish, a minister, beloved of his congregation and in harmony with his wealthy neighbours, could hope to receive a most handsome gift when some landmark in his career fell to be celebrated.

It was a matter of common occurrence also for a congregation to rise to great heights of generosity if their minister took ill. Long continental holidays for convalescence were financed at no expense to the invalids, and anything that money could buy which might aid recovery was provided. William Robertson of Irvine U.P. Church took seriously ill in 1871; to assist him back to health, he was provided with a free holiday and a gift of £5927 which was subscribed by just over 90 of his friends. The minister of Dingwall Free Church until 1884 was John Kennedy; on each occasion that he was forced to travel to improve his health, 'purses of gold were thrown at him'. At various times 'hundreds of guineas filled his lap from the hands of sympathetic admirers'. His biographer, Alexander Auld, sums up his good fortune in a nutshell when, speaking of Kennedy's hopes of wintering abroad one year, he remarks, 'The Lord, as He had often done previously, opened the way before him, and he was left without an anxious thought in pursuance of his purpose.' One would not immediately think of either Irvine or Dingwall as being centres of great wealth; one would hesitate to suggest that undeniably fine men like Robertson and Kennedy sought to curry favour with the well-to-do for selfish reasons. Nevertheless, inadequately though Scotland's ministers might be paid month by month, they could hope to have their financial position greatly improved if the right people in the parishes smiled their benediction on their labours. This must have gone some way at least to making ministers not exactly unwilling that the class structure should be retained. The ministry of George Morrison in Glasgow's Wellington Church was outwith the nineteenth century, but his experience shows how generous a prosperous congregation could be towards one who was a great minister and a good friend to them all. In 1919, he attained to his semi-jubilee in the ministry and received a gift of £500; the following year, he turned down a call to St. George's, Edinburgh, and was rewarded with a further £200 from a relieved congregation. In 1926, his congregation gave him over £400 to meet his expenses as Moderator of the United Free Church Assembly; £500 followed twelve months later when he celebrated 25 years in Wellington.

Chapter 10

Well done, thou good and faithful servant

The most significant area of change that overtook the life of the Scottish parish minister during the hundred year span of the nineteenth century would surely be found in the gradual decline, on almost all fronts, of his inbuilt authority and power. (There is, however, no implication that this was automatically detrimental either to his person, his message, or his Church.) The State took from him omnipotence in key aspects of education and welfare, and his parishioners, thanks to their own greater learning and travel, grew in independence and self-confidence to the point where they needed no longer to be in awe of his apparent omniscience. The minister's public pedestal was accordingly lowered, yet it is not in this area of influence that his condition was most changed. If he did not visibly sit on as many community thrones as did his predecessors, society was still anxious that he should be a major influence behind the new thrones, so that the parish minister in 1900 still found his opinion sought, and his friendship coveted to more or less the same extent as had his forbears a century before.

It is a rather different story, however, when we look at the measure of control he was able to exercise over the daily lives of his parishioners; here his effective authority did decline. In 1800, the kirk session still exercised its old privilege of summoning to its meetings those suspected of being involved in scandalous or immoral behaviour as well as those who had, without apparent satisfactory reason, absented themselves from public worship or violated the strict Sabbath code. Very early in the century, however, this practice was allowed to drop; the people of Scotland were becoming increasingly unwilling to submit to such courts, to suffer the ignominy of public reprimands, and to give their hard earned money to pay their fines. There was too the real question of whether more harm than good was being done by exposing innocent minds at Sunday worship to the detailed chronicle of misdemeanours of those being rebuked. Thus, the minister was 'stripped' of his former powers as judge in the session court.

For all that, however, many ministers for a time actually increased their ability to regulate what their people might do on the Sabbath. The Scottish minister's relation to Sabbath Observance is more complicated than is often realised. It is not the case that in this matter the Scottish Reformers set a high standard which was maintained generation after generation and only lowered in the last hundred years. On the contrary, the graph of observance fluctuated considerably over the centuries, and for a complete survey account would need to be taken of different generations, different ranks of society, different denominations and different parts of the country. The general reaction against the ideas of the French Revolution together with the strengthening of Evangelicalism in the churches led to an increasing stress on the Sabbath in the early decades of the nineteenth century. By 1830 the effects of eighteenth-century laxity had been neutralised except perhaps among the lowest ranks, and Sabbatarianism entered an aggressive phase which brought it into collision with trends of Victorian life such as the operating of Sunday trains. Except in certain districts Sabbatarianism in the Highlands and Islands was slower to develop with the result that it was coming to its peak in those parts during the second half of the century when in the Lowlands there was proceeding a general decline.

This aggressive Sabbatarianism, however, which was little removed from rank superstition in many ways, was not powered by the ministers alone; indeed, if there were ministers determined at all costs to keep the Sabbath Day utterly holy, there were not lacking those among the laity who would at once report to sessions and presbyteries any liberal-minded clergyman who appeared himself to be transgressing the Sabbath observance code. When, therefore, the graph of Sabbath Observance declined from its peak, it was due as much to a changing attitude on the part of many of the lay people as to a loss of control on the part of the clergy.

Ministers did, however, wield remarkable power as long as they were the recognised guardians of the Sabbath – the executives responsible for supervising that day's activities. Indeed, we can only wonder at the ordinary man's tolerance as harmless actions were declared forbidden. For example, in Thomas Guthrie's childhood, 'whistling was regarded as being as fit an occupation for the Lord's Day as profane swearing', and, incredible though it must appear, this ruling was held by the more zealous to be binding on the feathered kingdom also. Sir Archibald Geikie tells of one punctilious lady who rose specially early each Sunday morning so that she could carry down to the cellar her 'merry-hearted and loud-throated' canary to prevent its singing disturbing the solemnity of the hallowed day. Even more remarkable is the story told to Norman Macleod by Peter McKenzie, editor of the *Reformers' Gazette*. Early in the nineteenth century in Perth there was a kirk elder who kept birds, one of which, a starling, had a fine ear for old Scots tunes. One Sabbath, the minister passed by and heard it giving a fine rendering of 'Over the water to Charlie', a fact which so scandalised the holy man that he straight away ordered the elder to strangle the godless creature or demit his sacred office forthwith. To his eternal credit, the man chose to demit.

If there were no similarly outrageous stories authenticated elsewhere, such incidents could be dismissed as the eccentricities of the narrow-minded few, but the fact is that many similar tales can be told of ministers and laymen erecting immense barriers round the Sabbath Day and banning within the space of these sacred twenty-four hours anything that was not positively religious. For instance, the Rev. Duncan Mathieson, minister of Knock from 1831, suspended from Church membership for a year a teacher who was in training for the ministry because he had boarded the Monday morning boat for Skye late on the Sunday night. It was for the good of true religion when both minister and layman cooled down and began again to come to terms with a more liberal Sabbath. The evidence we have given thus far has been of clergymen condemning their parishioners, but the traffic was two-way. Early in the nineteenth century, several ministers ran into trouble for daring to shave on the Lord's Day; the Rev. Alexander Bower of Shiprow Relief Church in Aberdeen was actually taken to Presbytery by his managers in 1805 on this and similarly trivial charges, while the young Thomas Guthrie was given this advice on his first preaching trip to Ross-shire, 'Speak of shaving on the Lord's Day in

Ross-shire, and you need never preach here more.' Even as late as the 1920s, some earnest souls withdrew their membership from a Free Church in Skye when the minister's wife had the audacity to give birth to a son on the Sabbath: clearly the fourth commandment, in their eyes, was capable of expansion to include, 'Six days shalt thou be in labour.'

Intolerant Sabbatarianism was also affected by the vast amount of money invested in the expanding railway networks. The railway companies, not unnaturally, wished to reap the maximum revenue and this meant running Sunday trains. Without a doubt these Sunday services were well patronised: figures from 1842 show, for example, that as many as 900 passengers used the Sunday trains between Glasgow and Edinburgh. Agitation against them, however, gained momentum, and with the energies of such ministers as W. C. Burns and Murray McCheyne directed firmly in opposition, a certain amount of popular feeling was aroused. At the height of the controversy, many thousands thronged the railway stations in protest at the desecration of the Sabbath and joined in impressive acts of worship in the station forecourts. The upshot was that for the twenty-year period between 1846 and 1865, no trains were scheduled by the companies for the Sunday run from Glasgow to Edinburgh.

Similar campaigning, even to the Houses of Parliament, kept the public parks, gardens, art galleries and museums firmly closed to the public on Sundays, but such a negative approach could have no long-term future; nor could we wish it otherwise when we realise that the strict sabbatarian was motivated largely by a feeling of jealous apprehension. Such occupations as travelling by train or walking in pleasant surroundings were not regarded as inherently sinful, but the thought was that they would provide people with attractive alternative occupations for the Sunday and that the Churches would therefore be forsaken. In short, those urging the retention of the strict Sabbath wished the Church to have an absolute monopoly of all that could happen on a Sunday, recognising as they did 'that Church-going was too often indulged in, not as an act of devotion, but merely because there was no counter-attraction'. If the Church and her individual parish ministers lost a measure of power over their people with the liberating of the Sabbath, we can only agree that it was for the ultimate strength of the real Church, and we must greatly admire the courage of those prominent ministers who were prepared to take the lead and swim against the strong tide of Sabbatarianism. Norman Macleod, for instance, addressed Glasgow Presbytery for almost four hours on the subject of Sabbath Observance and declined to read from his pulpit that Presbytery's letter regarding Sunday trains; for his intelligent stand in this, he got abusive letters by the hundred and brother ministers shunned him in the street. Nevertheless, it is significant that he was not deposed; twenty years before this, he would have been. Principal Story, too, was a forthright champion of the more relaxed Sunday. Speaking at a Church Congress in Aberdeen in 1901, he said, 'Why leave those who do not go to Church no alternative resource of moral or spiritual benefit? I believe their religious life would not be hurt, and their health of body and mind would be promoted, if, on the Sunday afternoons, they found the parks and public gardens, the art galleries and libraries, freely open to them for their mental improvement and rational recreation.'

In certain areas, one is struck by the number of occasions in which powerful ministers were allowed an almost police-like authority within their parish areas. Understandably the eighteenth century saw more examples of this than the century which is our primary concern – James Robertson, minister of Lochbroom in the 1740s, for example, was 'reputed for checking with his fists his offending parishioners', while Mr. Pope, cousin of the poet and minister of Reay in Caithness, 'had a very feeling way of getting the people to Church: he clubbed them in and they dreaded his arm and his baton'. But the nineteenth century had its stalwarts whose disciplinary powers were not restricted only to the Sabbath. For instance, the Rev. Peter Maclean who died in 1868 was known as 'The Lion of the Lews': 'at nightfall, he would button his coat and wander through the streets to see that everything was in order; men in the public houses were afraid of him and tried to be home in good time. The sheriff said he was more to him than all the policemen, and he felt he could leave for holiday with an easy mind if Maclean were at home.' The Rev. Duncan Mathieson, whose grim views on the Sabbath we noted earlier, was another to be reckoned with. He was firmly of the opinion that dancing should not be permitted on any day of the week, and he had the utmost belief in his constabulary powers to prohibit it. In Gairloch, in the 1840s, a dance was secretly arranged. Mathieson, however, got news of it and he made for the Drill Hall, the scene of the outrage, armed with a stick. He threw open the door 'like an angel of judgment' and 'in a moment there was a stampede to the far end of the Hall and out, even though the organisers were not of his Church. The following Sunday he dealt with the dancers' sins, naming the families and itemising on them.' There was no public dance held in Gairloch for many years thereafter.

It is unhealthy in any democracy that a single individual should have the power forcibly to prohibit popular enjoyment of what is fully within the law of the land: it could do the Church no lasting credit that in a few parishes her leaders for a time claimed that power. It was a positive step forward when ministers realised that the respect of their people had to be won by their own quiet sincerity and dedication, and when obedience to their interpretation of God's will came spontaneously in love and not from fear. In the end of the day, the results were not always so very different. The elder Story in Rosneath was never the tyrant that Maclean or Mathieson was, but by his sheer personality and from the popular respect he had earned, he kept his parishioners in the straight and narrow: 'He was in the habit, if he saw a light in the village tavern on his return late at night from his perambulations in the parish, of going in and dismissing the company. Whenever he entered, there was a universal scuttle at the back door and the window for the privilege of being the first out of sight.'

A most welcome development in the life of the Scottish Church in the course of the nineteenth century – and no less welcome because it further modified the hold the ministers had over the affairs of their individual congregations – was the emergence of the lay leader to the point where the Church became more truly a partnership between the ordained and the lay. At the dawn of the nineteenth century, there was little scope for the enthusiastic layman within the established framework of the Church. Kirk Sessions were small in number and, with the loss of their former judicial powers, there was little of interest for them to do; even in Presbytery, the rule of strict parity between ordained and lay representatives operated only in theory, with few sessions troubling, or even being encouraged to send one of their number to the meetings.

This whole situation was mercifully to change during the nineteenth century, with the impetus coming from three different directions. In the first place, the Church itself so successfully widened the scope of its operations at parish level that ministers had to rely on lay office-bearers to carry the load. First off the ground were the Sunday schools which, once they gained official approval, proved so popular that lay teachers had to be enrolled. When, in the last quarter of the century there came into being such organisations as the Young Men's Guild, the Boys' Brigade, the Woman's Guild, the Christian Endeavour, the lay flood-gates were irreversibly opened for all time and the ministers acquired the role of adviser cum supervisor. Within the Church, too, there developed a growing awareness that the elders should have a more prominent part in the work of sessions and presbyteries. Thomas Guthrie was one who felt strongly on this, and he made a point of taking his representative elder with him to meetings of the Presbytery of Arbroath, a bold if legal step which, as Guthrie himself remarks, he took 'to the horror of the Moderate, and the terror of some of my timid Evangelical brethren'. Elsewhere, the forward-looking parish minister was increasing the size of his kirk session and giving the newly ordained an assortment of 'revolutionary' responsibilities covering district duties, teaching the young, and certain practical aspects of local social work. All this was a welcome far cry from the day when the session of a large congregation might number only half a dozen – when Norman Macleod was inducted to his first charge he found a session of just four – and when the purpose of their infrequent meetings was as often as not to rubber-stamp the wishes of their Moderator. In this regard the Rev. Dr. John Wilson, minister of Bellshill Relief Church from 1833 to 1884, was undoubtedly extreme, but he was not alone in his attitude even if his methods were unnecessarily obvious: 'He had always acted as clerk as well as Moderator of Session. Indeed, it is said that he usually went to the session meeting with the minute written out.' Prominent in the moves to elevate the lay power of the Church through more representative sessions and presbyteries were Thomas Guthrie, Norman Macleod, Thomas Chalmers, and Archibald Scott. Scott, in fact, captured the mood of such men when he said, 'I have set before myself the aim of getting every member of the congregation to do something on behalf of our work.'

The second factor which influenced the Church in Scotland to yield more to lay opinion was the national movement towards democracy which affected so many institutions in the nineteenth century. The Reform Act of 1832 showed the way, and the mood of the people was such that the Church could not expect to escape unscathed. The first great victory in the ecclesiastical sphere was the ending of the system of Patronage. With this change, the power of the lay member in the pew increased overnight; he now had a direct say in who would be his minister. While this need not in itself have weakened any minister's authority once appointed, subconsciously a minister could not but have felt that he owed it to his people to consult with them more readily than if he had been inducted through the power of the Patron. It would be wrong to exaggerate the effects of this; but as a by-product of the abolition of Patronage there were two developments which could further weaken a minister's hold over his parishioners. In the first place, ministers now no longer needed to await the smile of a Patron before considering a change of parish, and this, coupled with ever easier means of travel and communication, meant that the average ministry came to be of shorter duration than in former days. In the second place, where Patrons had frequently asked a son or nephew of the outgoing minister to fill the charge, congregations with a free choice were not so likely to cling to family ties. There was, then, less likelihood of any minister or related succession of ministers building up absolute control over how parishioners might think and react. A long ministry that was thoroughly good, or a 'royal family' in the manse that was both popular and efficient could be a great blessing in some particular parish, but on balance it was healthier that things should change as they did. Incidentally, there are some notable instances of fine 'family' ministries that succeeded. For example, for more than a hundred years, the parish of Strath in Skye was served by grandfather, father, and son of the Mackinnon family; in Morven, Norman Macleod's grandfather and uncle held the parish church for a hundred and seven years from 1775 to 1882; in St. Quivox, Ayrshire, father and son McQuhae ministered over the hundred year period to 1858, while we have already noted that in Rosneath the two Storys served with great distinction from 1815 to 1898.

Elsewhere within the Church, the popular urge for democracy was easily visible. Very naturally the Free Church was run on more democratic principles than had been the Established Church – the question of Patronage had, after all, been a key issue in the pre-Disruption struggles. The ministers who 'came out' in the Disruption owed a great deal to their people who were the source of their houses and stipends. The United Presbyterian Churches, too, operated on democratic lines, insisting on adequate lay representation in their Synod – in fact, they so valued the lay voice that congregations with more than four hundred members were allowed to send to that court not one but two elders.

Throughout Scotland, however, the growing love of democracy affected the Church most of all in the way that men and women began to question what earlier generations had been prepared to take on trust. Traditions, doctrines, the Scriptures and the very existence of God were openly debated by men and women who formerly would never have dared to utter a public word of criticism against either Church or minister. Able to think for themselves, willing to read for themselves, they more and more viewed fundamental debate with the clergy as their right, as the coming together of equals and not as an adult extension of the formal teacher/pupil relationship they had known in Sunday school. Anything the minister thus lost in personal authority was more than made good by the advent all around him of office-bearers and members for whom faith was a deliberate and knowledgeable choice.

The third element in the growing lay influence within the Church was the fact that increasingly there were devout laymen who were prepared to fight for and if necessary assume that measure of leadership within the Church which they felt should be theirs regardless of any opposition that might come from the clergy. Even in the early nineteenth century, for instance, there were still some examples of the 'praying societies' – groups of fervent laymen who met together for prayer and study and who were dissatisfied with the cold and rather barren state of the Moderate-controlled Church: such groups could possess very real powers in a community even to the stage of insisting on approving would-be members of the Church. More commonly associated with the nineteenth century, however, were 'The Men' whose activities have already been before us, and although in both cases this lay influence was largely restricted to the north and the remoter country areas, their achievements were none the less remarkable in the light of the inactive silence on the part of Scotland's laymen as a whole. Their members were certainly ahead of the organised Church and its ministers in their insistence that the laity had a right to be consulted in Church affairs.

On something like a nationwide scale, a powerful lay movement was experienced in the Churches in the Revivals of 1859–1860. As we saw, the real leaders of this series of revivals, and the main preachers at the revival meetings, were laymen. This in itself is surprising enough; it is even more surprising when we see the background of certain of these lay evangelists. Some were undoubtedly gentlemen of wealth and prestige, well educated and able to speak fluently to all classes: Brownlow North, Reginald Radcliffe and Hay Macdowall Grant, for example, would belong in this category. Others, however, came from the working classes and one or two had a dubious background. Robert Annan, for instance, was a runaway soldier, and Robert Cunningham was a prize-fighting butcher. Nevertheless, their preaching was listened to and it brought lasting results in many lives – a remarkable fact when in 1860 the lay voice was still muted in normal Church business.

The most striking example of a lead being taken by the laymen of Scotland to effect a radical change in official Church policy is seen in the growth of the Temperance Movement. Already we know of leading ministers who made it no secret that they greatly enjoyed a convivial glass of whatever was to hand – Carlyle and Webster were two who had little else in common. We noted too the clergy's collective enthusiasm for adequate beverages to soothe away the exhaustion of a Communion weekend: and from all this we could deduce, and deduce rightly, that early in the nineteenth century the Church in Scotland was far from supporting any doctrine of total abstinence. In the eighteenth and early nineteenth centuries, 'hard drinking was a habit in the most respectable circles and drunkenness was scarcely regarded as a sin'. In any kind of social get-together, a glass of whisky was then what a cup of tea is today, and the Church and her ministers for long felt no need to revise popular opinion in such matters. Indeed, there could be on occasion a definite link between the Church and alcohol. It was thought an advantage to have an inn near the church so that refreshment between the morning and afternoon services could easily be obtained. In the parish of Uig in Lewis in the 1820s, there was one person who was officially allowed to sell whisky outside the Church after each service; in the Secession Church of Cockburnspath which was opened in 1793, the beadle was licensed to sell ale in his house. According to one observer, this practice was wholly beneficial to the services of worship – 'They sang'd like Turks after it.'

The popular custom that a drink must accompany every event of any importance was solidly supported by ecclesiastical practice. Presbyterial dinners were assured of ample liquor through an elaborate system of fines; when a minister got a new manse, he was fined a bottle of wine; when he married, had a child, or had a sermon published, he was similarly penalised, as indeed he was if, attaining a certain age, he was still unmarried or still without children. Even religious ceremonies were thought to be more fittingly observed if all involved, including the ministers, partook of alcoholic refreshment. The elder Story's predecessor in Rosneath was Dr. Drummond. In his day, if the weather was cold at the time of the catechising, the elders would 'gently propose retiring to Jean's, the local public house'; likewise, at christenings, marriages and funerals, Jean received her full quota of ecclesiastical favours. Funerals provided the greatest opportunity for drinking to excess: 'respect for the dead was shown by the intoxication of the living', and there are cases recorded where funerals were postponed because the whisky had not arrived.

It was something of a rarity, therefore, to find any minister who practised or advocated total abstinence until as late as 1830. Thomas Guthrie states that while he was a student in the 1820s, there was not, so far as he knew, one abstaining minister in the whole Church. Guthrie himself was a total abstainer, perhaps the first great clerical figure to join the cause. Roderick Macleod of Snizort, the 'bishop' of Skye, was another who would not take alcohol, and later in the century Donald John Martin, John Cairns, and J. P. Struthers were three of the leaders of the Total Abstinence movement that was rapidly gaining ground. It was the laymen, however, who gave the real impetus to the movement. John Dunlop, a Greenock lawyer and elder, founded the Temperance Movement in Britain and, in the early stages, he had to face the fact that few clergymen would give him support. His first lecture, held in 1829, was not intimated from many pulpits, and it was only with great difficulty that he obtained a church in which the lecture could be delivered. By the end of 1830, however, a hundred societies had been formed in Scotland, and ministers had begun to take the issue seriously. The Free Church established a Temperance Committee in 1847: the Church of Scotland followed suit the following year: and by 1859, no less than 800 ministers were pledged to support the aims of the Society.

If the liberation of the Sabbath and the emancipation of the laity had the effect of reducing a minister's general parochial powers, there followed also real encouragement for the minister who was on top of his job, in that there emerged a new type of congregation in the pews week by week. They might number less than before; they would certainly be more critical than before; they were likely to demand a greater sense of involvement in the worship; but they were, more than formerly, genuine worshippers. It is all too easy to have in our minds an idyllic picture of worship in a Scots Church in those far-off days when everyone attended church and when the minister could prolong his pulpit exercises beyond three hours, knowing that next Sunday the same folk would be in the same places. It is too easy to assume that reverence, superstition and fear made these crowds into docile and attentive congregations. The people might attend because they thought they ought to or because they would have been even more bored staying at home, but in many parishes their behaviour presented an awesome challenge to the ordinary journeyman preacher. In the elder Story's biography we read this: 'The Sunday services not seldom extended over more than three hours. Long as it was, he expected all to remain to the close, and anyone who attempted to escape in the middle, as in the summer strangers would do, was sure to bring down on himself a reproof sharp and decisive. He kept in fact a tight rein of discipline over his congregation; any smiles, whispers, or apparent inattention were promptly checked, and all sleepers were awakened by a loud rap on the pulpit.' To take up just one point in that narrative, it would appear that Rosneath Kirk contained on occasion those who found it impossible to remain awake throughout the entire service; in this it was by no means unique. When John Caird was inducted to Newton-on-Ayr in 1845, he found that none of his predecessors had been able to stop certain of his congregation from 'resorting to somniferous oblivion the moment the preacher gave out the text'. Caird was a gifted preacher and he effected a considerable improvement, but to the end of his ministry in that Church, there remained one individual who staunchly upheld the old cutsom. A. K. H. Boyd had similar problems with his St. Andrews congregation: 'some human beings will not merely sleep but loudly evince that they are sleeping'. The more concerned ministers, of course, were alive to this type of situation, and they were not at a loss for dramatic remedies. Dr. Kidd of Gilcomston Chapel in Aberdeen, for example, kept a pocket Bible handily placed in the pulpit so that he could hurl it at any slumbering worshipper, accompanying it always with the quip, 'If he will not hear the Word of God, he will feel it.' The Rev. Alexander Campbell of Irvine Secession Church preferred to operate through the sleeper's neighbour who, in an imperious command from the pulpit, would be ordered to 'waken the sleeper'. Thereafter he would considerably recap his sermon for the benefit of the one who had missed part of it, and this in itself must greatly have encouraged the wakeful to keep a wary eye open for any drowsy colleagues so that they might be stirred to sufficient signs of life before the whole congregation was made thus to suffer for the indiscretions of the few.

If, however, there were those ministers who had trouble with those who would not keep awake, there were also occasional uneasy moments with those who were all too wide awake. The nineteenth century could boast nothing quite to equal the on-goings of the previous hundred years when, for example, in Keith, in 1723, some worshippers were fined in court for laughing and throwing clods and stones in Church, and for cutting and giving each other apples. There was, however, in Free St. John's, Edinburgh, during the ministry of Thomas Guthrie, a cattle-drover who, sitting right in front of the pulpit, passed the time by ostentatiously taking pinches of snuff. In Paisley Abbey, Cameron Lees, who was there from 1859 to 1877, had this to endure in the course of his morning service: 'There were stoves in the outer passage and when I was preaching I have seen people come in and take a turn round the stoves and listen for a while and just walk out again. I have seen a man come to the stove right in front of the pulpit, take out his pipe, fill it, light it, see if it drew, and then walk out.' Even more daring were the old wives who lined the pulpit stairs in Old Greyfriars, Edinburgh, during the ministry of Dr. Erskine who died in 1803. Time and again they cleverly removed his pocket handkerchief as he passed through their midst, with the result that his wife had eventually to stitch one in place, to the annoyance and embarrassment of her who gave it the accustomed deft tug the following Sunday.

There will always be those who attend Church without being in earnest about the worship; there will always be those whose attention will momentarily wander or whose fidgets will distract their neighbours, but as the nineteenth century wore on, the ministers found less of this nature to contend with as a new spirit of honest devotion more than compensated for the rather emptier pews. Even at that, however, few worshippers were prepared to go to the lengths of one precentor quoted by Elizabeth Haldane: so anxious was he that he should always be alert and attentive that he regularly sat through the service with a piece of holly concealed under his chin.

With the advent of the more attentive and better educated congregation, the Church Service itself took on a more orderly appearance and called for more active involvement on the part of the worshippers. For example, after some stormy debates, hymns and organs were introduced: hitherto, only two or at most three psalms had been 'droned' in any one service, with precentors frequently having a very limited range of tunes in their repertoire. (Norman Macleod quotes one who knew not more than four.) The reading of the Scriptures, too, came to be a regular feature of public worship; prior to an injunction of the General Assembly in 1856 this was a practice which 'was almost universally neglected'. The congregation also came to have a vocal part in the prayers with the gradual introduction of the repetition of the Lord's Prayer. There is the immortal tale of Dr. Lamont, Moderator of the General Assembly in 1822, being taken up a close in Edinburgh by Dr. Inglis, minister of Greyfriars, so that he could be taught this prayer for use in a service to be attended by George IV. Most important of all, the sermons, which had formerly been judged on length, fluency, and absence of notes, came now to be marked by reasoned argument and intelligibility. Principal Caird was a fine preacher even if on occasion he over-estimated the intellectual abilities of his hearers: 'Was he no' graun' the day?', remarked one elderly worshipper to another as they left his Errol Kirk. 'Ay, but did ye understaun' him?' was the response. 'Understaun' him?' echoed the first speaker; 'I wadna presoom.' So it had been for many a day in Scottish kirks, but standards were changing and there was to be no going back. (At the same time, it must not be imagined that all these changes were easily introduced: we remarked that it took some stormy debates to have organs accepted in worship; a measure of the hostility to instrumental music in the service of God is seen in the arguments that raged in a Roxburghshire Church when a new heating stove was proposed. No one doubted the need of additional or improved heat in Church: no one questioned the efficiency of the boiler advocated; the difficulty was the fact that the stove had a pipe like an organ pipe and this was sufficient to delay the project for some considerable time.)

From all that has gone before, one inescapable conclusion has to be drawn: whether we look at 1800 or 1900 or at any date in between, the dedicated amongst the clergy of Scotland had more than sufficient in the way of necessary duty to keep them thoroughly busy. Regardless of their denomination, their particular parochial powers, or the number of lay leaders at their disposal, there was in the work of preaching, visiting and community affairs more than ample occupation for all the working hours of a week. We surely can say also, that, on the whole, Scotland's ministers in the nineteenth century carried out their duties every bit as conscientiously as had any of their predecessors. The invalid Murray McCheyne said that he wanted 'a short life in the saddle rather than a long life by the fire'; Robert Burns's wife records that her husband was constantly busy but that he would not have been happy otherwise; W. C.

Burns frequently expressed the hope that his mother would be right and that he would be a 'knife worn out by cutting and not by rusting'. Such remarks are typical of the vast majority of their colleagues and Scotland has every right to feel proud of them.

There were those who were inefficient and lazy – there always will be. The Church in Scotland was frequently torn by internal division and dissension in the century we have been reviewing – we have not tried to hide this. The unsavoury is there if we wish to uncover it – copies of the *Glasgow Herald* for the second half of 1873 show a minister involved in a divorce case, two ministers under investigation for alleged unlawful dealing over a will, yet another clergyman accused of falsehood and perjury, and an English vicar charged with drunkenness and immorality. There are former manse servants still alive who can tell stories of uncertain temper on the part of ecclesiastical giants at the turn of the century which never found their way into books of memoirs. We can extract from various sources references to clergymen who had their strange ways – Lachlan Mackenzie, for example, minister of Lochcarron from 1782 to 1819, preached one hot summer day wearing three vests, two coats, an overcoat, and a cloak: Norman Macleod's mother tells of a clergyman, minister of Knapdale, who, when he preached, 'wore a white cotton night-cap': William Dunn, minister in Cardross from 1838 to 1881, was never known to preach without his stiff grey kid gloves. So we could have proceeded, unearthing and highlighting the eccentric and the unsavoury, but this would have been totally untrue to the ordained Churchman of the nineteenth century.

Epilogue

We can but hope that you have found this book as absorbing in the reading as the author found it in the compiling. There have been, perhaps, those sidelights and snapshots that astonished and surprised. And yet, have we not come nearer the heartbeat of a mighty Scots tradition, as together we followed the Auld Scots Minister in his study, his home, his flock, his parish, his day and generation?

Principal Rainy tells of a girl he met on holiday: she was, he said, 'oppressed with the Scottish respect for all who mount pulpits'. Maybe so; but during the course of the nineteenth century, this respect, where it truly mattered, was not noticeably diminished, even although the superficial hold of the Church was apparently weakened. After meditating and reflecting on the story of these pages, we are convinced that this respect was in the main truly justified, and was the foundation of the real respect with which the Church of our own twentieth century is still regarded by our own Scottish people.

Select Bibliography

THOMAS ADAMSON: *Free Anderston Church, Glasgow*: Glasgow – Maclure, Macdonald: 1900

ROBERT ANDERSON: *A History of Kilsyth and a Memorial of two lives*: Kilsyth – J. M. Duncan: 1901

WILLIAM ANDREWS: *Bygone Church life in Scotland*: London – William Andrews: 1899

ANON.: *Horatius Bonar: a memorial*: London – James Nisbet: 1889

ANON.: *John Buchan* (1847–1911): Peebles – Privately printed: 1912

ANON.: *Discourses of the Rev. Stevenson MacGill with Memoir*: Glasgow – Bell and Bain: 1844

ANON.: *Memorials of the late Rev. Christopher Munro*: Edinburgh – Macniven and Wallace: 1890

ANON.: *James Robertson of Newington*: Edinburgh – Andrew Elliot: 1887

WILLIAM ARNOT: *Life of James Hamilton*: London – James Nisbet: 1870

ALEXANDER AULD: *Life of John Kennedy*: London – T. Nelson: 1887

THE LADY FRANCES BALFOUR: *Life and letters of the Rev. James MacGregor*: London – Hodder and Stoughton: 1912

JAMES BANNERMAN: *The Church of Christ*: two volumes: Edinburgh – T. and T. Clark: 1868

G. F. BARBOUR: *The Life of Alexander Whyte*: London – Hodder and Stoughton: 1923

PETER BAYNE: *The life and letters of Hugh Miller*: (two volumes): London – Strahan: 1871

JOHN S. BLACK & GEORGE CHRYSTAL: *The Life of William Robertson Smith*: London – Adam and Charles Black: 1912

W. G. BLAIKIE: *After fifty years*: London – Thomas Nelson: 1893

—— *Recollections of a busy life: autobiography*: edited by Norman L. Walker: London – Hodder and Stoughton: 1901

—— *The preachers of Scotland from 6th to 19th century*: Edinburgh – T. and T. Clark: 1888.

—— *For the work of the ministry*: London – Daldy, Isbister: 1874

ANDREW A. BONAR: *Memoir and Remains of Rev. Robert Murray McCheyne*: Edinburgh – Oliphant, Anderson and Ferrier: 1844

HORATIUS BONAR: *Life of the Rev. John Milne*: London – James Nisbet: 1868

MARJORY BONAR: *Andrew A. Bonar: Diary and Letters*: London – Hodder and Stoughton: 1893

—— *Reminiscences of Andrew A. Bonar*: London – Hodder and Stoughton: 1895

A. K. H. Boyd: *The Lessons of Middle Age*: London – Longmans, Green: 1869

—— *The Recreations of a Country Parson*: second series: London, Longmans, Green: 1866

—— *Sunday afternoons at the Parish Church of a University City*: London – Longmans, Green: 1867

—— *Twenty Five years of St. Andrews*: two volumes: third edition: London – Longmans, Green: 1892

James Brown: *Life of John Eadie*: London – MacMillan: 1878

—— *Life of William B. Robertson of Irvine*: Glasgow – James Maclehose: 1888

—— *The Life of a Scottish Probationer*: Glasgow – James Maclehose: 1878

John Brown: *Horae Subsecivae*: three volumes: London – Adam and Charles Black: 1897

Thomas Brown: *Annals of the Disruption*: Edinburgh – Macniven and Wallace: 1884

J. H. S. Burleigh: *A Church History of Scotland*: London – Oxford University Press: 1960

Islay Burns: *Memoir of Rev. William C. Burns*: London – James Nisbet: 1869

James C. Burns: *Select Remains of Islay Burns*: London – James Nisbet: 1874

Robert Burns: *Memoir of the Rev. Stevenson MacGill*: Edinburgh – John Johnstone: 1842

R. F. Burns: *Life and times of Robert Burns of Paisley: with unfinished biography*: Toronto – J. Campbell: 1872

J. H. Burton (editor): *Autobiography of Rev. Dr. Alexander Carlyle*: Edinburgh – William Blackwood: 1860

John Caird: *University Sermons (Glasgow)*: Glasgow – James Maclehose 1898

David S. Cairns: *Life and times of Alexander Robertson MacEwen*: London – Hodder and Stoughton: 1925

John Cairns: *Memoir of John Brown*: Edinburgh – Thomas Constable: 1860

George G. Cameron: *Memorials of John Roxburgh*: Glasgow – David Bryce: 1881

A. J. Campbell: *Two centuries of the Church of Scotland: 1701–1929*: Paisley – Alexander Gardner: 1930

Donald Campbell: *Memorials of John Mcleod Campbell*: two volumes: London – Macmillan: 1877

R. S. Candlish: *Sermons, with biographical preface*: Edinburgh – Adam and Charles Black: 1873

Thomas Cassels: *Men of the knotted heart*: Greenock – James McKelvie: 1915

A. H. Charteris: *A faithful Churchman: Memoir of James Robertson*: Edinburgh: R. and R. Clark: 1897

—— *The Church of Christ: its life and work*: Baird Lecture for 1887: London – Macmillan: 1905

John Cunningham: *The Church History of Scotland*: two volumes: second edition: Edinburgh – James Thin: 1882

T. H. Darlow: *William Robertson Nicoll: Life and letters*: London – Hodder and Stoughton: 1925

JAMES DENNEY: *Letters to William Robertson Nicoll: 1893–1917*: London – Hodder and Stoughton: 1920

JOHN DICKSON: *Cranstoun – a Parish History*: Anstruther – Privately printed: 1907

MARCUS DODS: *Early letters of Marcus Dods: 1850–1864*: London – Hodder and Stoughton: 1910

—— *Later letters of Marcus Dods: 1895–1909*: London – Hodder and Stoughton: 1911

GEORGE JOHN C. DUNCAN: *Memoir of Rev. Henry Duncan*: Edinburgh – William Oliphant: 1848

Evangelical Magazine: Issues for 1810, 1811, 1822

PATRICK FAIRBAIRN: *Pastoral Theology*: Edinburgh: 1875

FERGUS FERGUSON: *The life of the Rev. Andrew A. Bonar*: Glasgow – John J. Rae: no date

J. R. FLEMING: *A History of the Church in Scotland*: Vol 1: 1843–1874; Vol 2: 1875–1929: Edinburgh – T. and T. Clark: 1927 and 1933

—— *The Burning Bush*: Edinburgh – T. and T. Clark: 1913

J. G. FYFE: *Scottish Diaries and Memoirs: 1746–1843*: Stirling – Eneas Mackay: 1942

JOHN GALT: *Annals of the Parish*: London – T. N. Foulis: 1910

ALEXANDER GAMMIE: *The Churches of Aberdeen: Historical and Descriptive*: Aberdeen – Daily Journal Office: 1909

—— *Dr. Archibald Fleming of St. Columba's*: London – James Clarke: 1932

—— *Dr. George H. Morrison: the man and his work*: London – James Clarke: 1928

SIR ARCHILBALD GEIKIE: *Scottish Reminiscences*: Glasgow – James Maclehose: 1904

ALEXANDER GERARD: *The Pastoral Care*: London – G. Gerard: 1799

REV. THE HON. ARTHUR GORDON: *Life of Archibald Hamilton Charteris*: London – Hodder and Stoughton: 1912

WILLIAM GRAHAM (editor): *Andrew Somerville: an autobiography*: Edinburgh – Macniven and Wallace: 1880

JOHN GREIG: *Disruption Worthies of the Highlands: another memorial*: Edinburgh – John Greig 1877

ARTHUR GUTHRIE: *Robertson of Irvine: poet preacher*: Ardrossan – Arthur Guthrie: 1890

DAVID K. GUTHRIE & CHARLES J. GUTHRIE: *Autobiography of Thomas Guthrie and Memoir*: (two volumes): London – W. Isbister: 1873 and 1876

ELIZABETH S. HALDANE: *The Scotland of our Fathers*: London – Alexander Maclehose: 1933

JAMES J. Hunter: *Historical notices of Lady Yester's Church and Parish*: Edinburgh – Johnstone, Hunter: 1864

JOHN A. IRELAND: *A legacy from a Scottish manse*: London – Hodder and Stoughton: 1918

James C. IRONS: *Memorial of a faithful ministry: The life and work of the Rev. David Irons*: Glasgow – W. and R. Holmes: 1909

DAVID JAMIE: *John Hope: Philanthropist and Reformer*: Edinburgh – Andrew Elliot: 1900

CHARLES JERDAN: *Scottish clerical stories and reminiscences*: Edinburgh – Oliphants 1920

JOHN KENNEDY: *The Life and labours of the Rev. Dr. McDonald – The Apostle of the North*: London – T. Nelson: 1866

R. S. KIRKPATRICK: *John Macleod in the parish of Govan*: Edinburgh – W. Blackwood: 1915

WILLIAM KNIGHT: *Some 19th century Scotsmen*: Edinburgh – Oliphant, Anderson and Ferrier: 1903

P. LANDRETH: *Life and ministry of the Rev. Adam Thomson of Coldstream*: Edinburgh – Andrew Elliot: 1869

W. KEITH LEASK: *Dr. Thomas McLauchlan*: Edinburgh – Oliphant, Anderson and Ferrier: 1905

PRINCIPAL T. M. LINDSAY: *College Addresses and Sermons*: Glasgow – J. Maclehose: 1915

A. R. MACEWEN: *Life and letters of John Cairns*: London – Hodder and Stoughton: 1895

NORMAN C. MACFARLANE: *Rev. Donald John Martin: preacher, soul winner, social reformer*: Edinburgh – Oliphant, Anderson and Ferrier: (paperback) 1914

—— *Apostles of the North*: Stornoway – The Gazette Office: no date

DUNCAN CAMPBELL MACGREGOR: *George H. C. Macgregor: a biography*: London – Hodder and Stoughton: 1900

JOHN MACINNES: *The Evangelical Movement in the Highlands of Scotland: 1688–1800*: Aberdeen – The University Press: 1951

JOHN MACKAY: *The Church in the Highlands*: London – Hodder and Stoughton: 1914

ELLA S. MACKENZIE: *The Rev. Murdo Mackenzie: a memory*: Inverness – Robert Carruthers: 1914

ROBERT MACKENZIE: *John Brown of Haddington*: London – The Banner of Truth Trust: (paperback) 1964

KENNETH MCLAREN: *Memoir of the Very Rev. Professor Charteris*: London – Adam and Charles Black: 1914

NORMAN MACLEAN: *The life of James Cameron Lees*: Glasgow – Maclehose, Jackson: 1922

DONALD MACLEOD: *Memoir of Norman Macleod*: (two volumes): London – Daldy, Isbister: 1876

NORMAN MACLEOD: *Reminiscences of a Highland Parish*: London – S. W. Partridge: no date

D. MACMILLAN: *The life of George Matheson*: London – Hodder and Stoughton: 1907

JOHN MACPHERSON: *A History of the Church in Scotland*: Paisley – Alexander Gardner: 1901

STEWART MECHIE: *Education for the Ministry in Scotlamd since the Reformation*: Three Parts: Contained in the *Records of the Scottish Church History Society*: Volume 14, part 2: volume 14, part 3: volume 15, part 1: 1961–1963

—— *The Church and Scottish Social Development: 1780–1870*: London – Oxford University Press: 1960

JAMES MITCHELL: *Some Annals of Wellington Street Church*: Glasgow – Aird and Coghill: 1877

KENNETH MOODY-STUART: *Brownlow North: Records and Recollections*: London – Hodder and Stoughton: 1878

—— *Alexander Moody Stuart: a Memoir*: London – Hodder and Stoughton: 1899

A. D. MORRISON: *The Story of Free St. David's, Kirkintilloch*: Privately published: 1926

CHRISTINE M. MORRISON: *Morrison of Wellington*: London – Hodder and Stoughton: 1928

EUNICE G. MURRAY: *The Church of Cardross and its ministers*: Glasgow – Jackson: 1935

W. ROBERTSON NICOLL: *'Ian Maclaren': Life of the Rev. John Watson*: London – Hodder and Stoughton: 1908

—— *My father: an Aberdeenshire minister*: London – Hodder and Stoughton: 1908

MRS. OLIPHANT: *Thomas Chalmers*: London – Methuen: 1893

—— *The life of Edward Irving*: London – Hurst and Blackett: no date

—— *Memoir of the life of John Tulloch*: Edinburgh – William Blackwood: 1888

ADAM PHILIP: *Thomas Chalmers: Apostle of Union*: London – James Clarke: 1929

J. BOYD PRIMMER: *Life of Jacob Primmer*: Edinburgh – William Bishop: 1916

JAMES PRIMROSE: *The mother anti-burgher Church of Glasgow*: Glasgow – Blackie: 1896

JAMES PRINGLE: *The story of West St. Giles Parish Church*: Edinburgh – William Blackwood: 1916

JOHN REITH: *Life and writings of Rev. Alex. Murray*: Dumfries – J. Maxwell: 1903

J. M. E. ROSS: *William Ross of Cowcaddens: a memoir*: London – Hodder and Stoughton: 1905

DONALD SAGE: *Memorabilia Domestica: or Parish life in the north of Scotland*: Wick – William Rae: 1889

THE ST. GILES LECTURES: first series: *The Scottish Church from the earliest times to 1881*: Edinburgh – W. and R. Chambers: 1881

—— third series: *Scottish Divines*: Edinburgh – Macniven and Wallace: 1883

—— sixth series: *The Church and the people*: Edinburgh – Macniven and Wallace: 1886

THE HON. LORD SANDS: *Dr. Archibald Scott of St. George's, Edinburgh, and his times*: Edinburgh – William Blackwood: 1919

—— *The story of St. Stephen's, Edinburgh*: Edinburgh – William Blackwood: 1927

—— *The life of Andrew Wallace Williamson*: Edinburgh – William Blackwood 1929

P. CARNEGIE SIMPSON: *The life of Principal Rainy*: (two volumes): London – Hodder and Stoughton: 1909

OLIPHANT SMEATON: *Principal James Morison: the man and his work*: Edinburgh – Oliver and Boyd:1902

ALEXANDER SMELLIE: *Robert Murray McCheyne*: London – National Council of Evangelical Free Churches: 1913
GEORGE ADAM SMITH: *The life of Henry Drummond*: London – Hodder and Stoughton: 1899
SYDNEY SMITH: *Donald Macleod of Glasgow: a memoir and a study*: London – James Clarke: 1926
THOMAS SMITH: *Memoirs of James Begg*: with autobiographical chapters: two volumes: Edinburgh – J. Gemmell: 1885/1888
A. N. SOMERVILLE: *Precious seed sown in many lands: sermons with biographical sketch*: London – Hodder and Stoughton: 1890
JAMES STARK: *Dr. Kidd of Aberdeen*: Aberdeen – D. Wyllie: 1898
JANE T. STODDART: *W. Robertson Nicoll: editor and preacher*: London – S. W. Partridge 1903
J. L. STORY: *Early Reminiscences*: Glasgow – James Maclehose: 1911
—— *Later Reminiscences*: Glasgow – James Maclehose: 1913
THE MISSES STORY: *Memoir of Robert Herbert Story*: Glasgow – James Maclehose 1909
ROBERT HERBERT STORY: *Memoir of the life of the Rev. Robert Story*: Cambridge – Macmillan: 1911
A. L. STRUTHERS: *Life and letters of John Paterson Struthers*: London – Hodder and Stoughton: no date
ARTHUR P. SYM: *The parish of Lilliesleaf*: Selkirk – James Lewis: 1913
JAMES TAIT: *Two centuries of Border Church Life*: two volumes: Kelso – J. and J. H. Rutherfurd: 1889 and 1891
P. D. THOMSON: *Parish and Parish Church*: The Baird Lecture 1935: London – Thomas Nelson: 1948
W. R. THOMSON: *The first Relief Church in the West*: Glasgow – John Smith: 1913
JOSEPH J. WALKER: *Fountainhall Road Church, Edinburgh*: Edinburgh – Oliver and Boyd: 1929
NORMAN L. WALKER: *Chapters from the History of the Free Church of Scotland*: Edinburgh – Oliphant, Anderson and Ferrier: 1895
CHARLES L. WARR: *Principal Caird*: Edinburgh – T. and T. Clark: 1926
—— *Alfred Warr of Rosneath*: Paisley – Alexander Gardner: 1917
JEAN L. WATSON: *Life of Dr. Andrew Thomson*: Edinburgh – J. Gemmell: 1882
HUGH WATT: *Thomas Chalmers and the Disruption*: Edinburgh – Thomas Nelson: 1943
SIR HENRY MONCREIFF WELLWOOD: *Account of the life and writings of John Erskine*: Edinburgh – Archibald Constable: 1818
JOHN WILSON: *Narrative of the origin and progress of the Relief Church, Bellshill*: Glasgow – S. and T. Dunn: 1848
WILLIAM WILSON: *Memorials of Robert Smith Candlish*: Edinburgh – Adam and Charles Black: 1880
RONALD SELBY WRIGHT: *Fathers of the Kirk*: London – Oxford University Press: 1960
—— *The Kirk in the Canongate*: Edinburgh – Oliver and Boyd: 1956
JAMES A. WYLIE: *Disruption Worthies: a memorial of 1843*: Edinburgh – Thomas C. Jack: no date

Index